The Future of the Family

The Future of the Family

by

WENDY GREEN

MOWBRAY
LONDON & OXFORD

First published 1984
by A.R. Mowbray & Co. Ltd,
Saint Thomas House, Becket Street,
Oxford, OX1 1SJ

Typeset by Oxford Computer Typesetting
and printed in Great Britain by
Spottiswoode Ballantyne Ltd, Colchester.

British Library Cataloguing in Publication Data

Green, Wendy
   The future of the family.
   1. Family — Religious life
   I. Title
   261.8'3585   BV4526.2

   ISBN 0-264-66824-3

Contents

Acknowledgements

I would like to express my thanks to all who have contributed their time and expertise to the shaping of this book, and also to the following for permission to reproduce material of which they are the authors, publishers or copyright holders.

Jonathan Cape Limited for an extract from *The Subversive Family* by Ferdinand Mount.

Darton, Longman & Todd Limited for extracts from *Marriage, Faith and Love* by Dr Jack Dominian, published and copyright 1981 by Darton, Longman & Todd Limited, London.

David Higham Associates Limited on behalf of Victor Gollancz Ltd and the estate of Dorothy L. Sayers for an extract from *Unpopular Opinions* by Dorothy L. Sayers.

Victor Gollancz Ltd and Betty Friedan for an extract from *The Feminine Mystique* by Betty Friedan.

Michael Joseph Ltd for an extract from *The Second Stage* by Betty Friedan.

The Macmillan Press Limited for extracts from *A Fairer Future for Children* by Mia Kellmer Pringle.

National Children's Bureau for extracts from *Parenting Papers*.

Office of Population Censuses and Surveys.

Penguin Books Ltd for two extracts from *The Family and Marriage in Britain* by Ronald Fletcher (Pelican Books, Third Edition 1973), copyright © Ronald Fletcher, 1962, 1966, 1973.

Random House, Inc. for extracts from *Ourselves and our children: a book by and for parents* by The Boston Women's Health Book Collective.

Routledge & Kegan Paul for extracts from *Fathers, Mothers and Others* by Rapoport and Rapoport (1978) and from *Working Couples* by Rapoport and Rapoport (1978).

David Higham Associates Limited on behalf of Routledge & Kegan Paul for an extract from *Webs of Violence* by Jean Renvoize.

The Study Commission on the Family for extracts from *Families in Focus* by Lesley Rimmer and *Happy Families*.

SCM Press Ltd for extracts from *Dispossessed Daughters of Eve* by Susan Dowell and Linda Hurcombe.

Virago Press Ltd for an extract from *Testament of Friendship* by Vera Brittain first published by Macmillan & Co. Ltd, reprinted by Virago Ltd, 1980; copyright Vera Brittain 1940; and for an extract by George Fox quoted in *Not in God's Image* by Julia O'Faolain and Lauro Martines, first published by Virago, 1979.

World Council of Churches Publications Office, Geneva for an extract from *Sexism in the 1900s: Discrimination against Women*.

Argus Communications for material from *Why Marriage* by Edward E. Ford and Robert L. Zorn, © 1974 Argus Communications, a division of DLM, Inc., Allen, TX 75002.

W.G.

Foreword

I am confident that our survival depends increasingly on the survival of family life in the UK — not necessarily life in isolated nuclear family units but in groups where children are nurtured by a husband and wife who are committed to one another for life.

The terrifying toll on family life in Britain in the last decade, so that one in seven families is now headed by a single parent is showing itself in lives of adults and of children who are wounded and desperately in need of deep healing. The many hours I have spent talking to men and women whose broken marriages have shattered their lives, and the agony through which they have passed, are enough to convince me that Wendy Green's book is important and significant.

She has amassed and read a vast amount of current literature on the woman's movement and family life today both from the serious press and from popular magazines, and presents her findings of what is happening to family life, and why, in a concise manner. We are in her debt for reading on our behalf all those books we ought to read, but do not have time to!

Her book makes solemn reading, since it cannot be read as an academic exercise. To read a book like this, to absorb what it is saying, must for the Christian be a challenge and a call to practical action. As Wendy points out, the Church is doing very little about this major area of need in the life of our nation today.

For many of us, ignorance is the cause of our indifference — once we know about situations, and are challenged to pray about them, for many of us comes the call of God: 'Go, and be the answer to your own prayers by doing something yourself!'.

It is my sincere prayer that theological students, Bible college students, parish priests and church workers will read this book with open hearts and be ready when God says, 'Who shall we send and who will go for us?' to respond as Isaiah did with the words, 'Lord, here am I, send me!'.

Anne J. Townsend
Director of CARE Trust,
and former editor of *Family* magazine

Introduction

When I was asked to write this book I was already aware of the pressures some families are having to face. As the research material accumulated, and the complexity of the problems became more apparent, I began to wonder not so much if there is a future for the family but how some families manage to survive at all.

There are so many factors threatening, undermining and devaluing individuals, and the way they relate to the other individuals in their social unit. In many ways this book only scratches the surface. Each section merits a book, or several books, of its own.

I make no claim to instant answers. I can only spell out the kind of tensions that are placing families 'at risk'. No one will be able to change the situation overnight, or even in the next decade, but we could start asking the questions, or listening to the questions others are asking that might begin to shed some glimmers of light on certain areas.

It is not by accident that the chapters on women and work, and feminism, are much longer than the others. From the start it was obvious that these two issues were central. The options open to women have widened so enormously this century. Their expectations and evaluation of themselves have altered accordingly. We are still in the process of waking up to how this is altering the male/female relationship which is at the heart of most family units.

Tensions and misunderstandings have been inevitable, especially where communication is poor, or there has been reluctance to think through a constructive response. Traditional roles, stereotypes, and familiar assumptions are all under attack. The future could be a time of negotiation, re-discovery and reconciliation as men and women work out

1

the patterns and lifestyles which are most appropriate to their circumstances, or it could result in continuing alienation, and disintegration.

There is an urgent need for education in the basic skills and discipline necessary when relating to an other/others. An enormous number of people will need encouragement, the patterns and lifestyles which are most appropriate to their circumstances, or it could result in continuing alienation, and disintegration.

There is an urgent need for education in the basic skills and discipline necessary when relating to an other/others. An enormous number of people will need encouragement, affirmation, the knowledge that they are of worth. Someone remarked recently that Jesus taught very little about marriage. I don't think he needed to. His teaching was all about priorities, relationships, the value we place on the other person, our answerability to one another, and to God. If we could plug that kind of power into our teaching, preaching, counselling and most importantly, the place where we have *most* influence, our families, maybe we would begin to make some impact as salt and light to our very needy world.

1

A changing world

Four couples sat relaxing after an enjoyable meal. 'What's your latest book about?' one of the men asked. 'Is there a future for the family?' I replied. 'Surely that can't be seriously in doubt,' he said disparagingly. The others nodded their agreement.

End of discussion.

That experience was not unique. I have met similar reactions since, especially in Christian circles. It seems as if Christians have a particular facility for imagining that if they ignore, or denounce certain unpalatable truths they will disappear. Unfortunately, as with unemployment, some of the statistics about family life are going to need far more than wishful thinking if there is to be any impact upon them.

Sobering statistics
The media men may still sell the traditional image of the family: mum, dad and one or two delightful children. Behind the gloss, the cameras, the synthetic smiles an increasing number have 'given up' on the family. In 1979 only one-third of households were made up of two parents and their dependent children. If you pursue the image to its ultimate form and think in terms of mother staying at home to care for the children the figure drops to 15 per cent.

'You can no longer suggest that children should make a card for Father's Day,' sighed a despairing teacher, 'And getting the right surname on letters home is a nightmare.'

Family patterns
In many ways the traditional nuclear family is becoming an endangered species. The couples who dismissed any suggestion that the family was under threat need have

looked no further than their own circle of acquaintances to
see how diverse family patterns have become. Family units
today may consist of one parent plus children, couples
choosing not to have children, couples 'living together',
people living in community, the extended family groups of
the ethnic minorities, and reconstituted or blended
families, following a remarriage. Even the 'traditional'
family may be very different from the usual picture of mum
at the kitchen sink and dad as the breadwinner. Unemployment, women's liberation, and an increased number of
women in paid employment have all contributed to a situation where jobs and roles may be shared, or even reversed.
Individual units may be small and isolated but with the
proportion of elderly and very elderly increasing there will
also be an increase in four generation families.

Social changes

For those steeped in literature, including the Bible, such
diversity of relationships and family organization will come
as no surprise. People are different. Their values and
attitudes differ. They do not react uniformly to the situations in which they find themselves. Social conditions alter.
Families adapt accordingly.

The problem in this century is that things have changed
so rapidly that all of us have difficulty appreciating, let
alone coming to terms with, the various factors which have
had such enormous influences on family life. My father-in-
law, born at the turn of the century, lived in an isolated rural
community, dependent on horses or feet for transport and
communication. My children hardly turn a hair at the sight
of the spaceshuttle piggy-backing on a jumbo jet over our
multi-racial inner city neighbourhood. Nobody questioned
the propriety of grandad climbing into bed to comfort his
three girl cousins in a thunderstorm when they were teenagers. When my eldest daughter shares a bed top to tail with
her schoolmate, her twelve year old sister accuses her of
being a 'homo sapiens'. Granny and grandad both came
from families with seven or eight children. Our four are
regarded as a large family now the national average is 1.7

children per family. In five or six years' time my mother could find herself a great-grandmother, and still live ten or fifteen years to enjoy her great-grandchildren. If she had been born a few decades earlier she would have been lucky to have survived beyond her fiftieth birthday. When she was a child, women were still fighting for the vote and the first birth control clinics were receiving strong opposition. Nowadays children receive sex education in school and when I became pregnant with our fourth child the first option offered to me was an abortion.

Change in the balance of power

Smaller families, more job opportunities for women, the relaxation of the divorce laws and the influence of the women's liberation movement have all contributed to the most radical change in family life this century — a shift in the balance of power in male/female relationships. Church leaders may denounce the fact, the average male deplore it, but modern women are not only insisting that they are equal, if not superior, to men, they are at long last able to survive independently.

'It's like a canker at the heart of the relationship', one man growled. 'If she says "I'm going" you can no longer call her bluff.' He seemed oblivious of the fact that for centuries women have experienced very similar feelings, but in reverse.

The permissive society

Now that there is a choice is it really surprising that so many are opting out of difficult situations when the predominant messages of recent years have been 'do your own thing, don't worry about the consequences, as long as you get satisfaction — particularly sexual satisfaction'?

The media must bear a terrific burden of responsibility for 'popularizing' the permissive society. The amoral goings on of *Dallas* or *Dynasty* may appear to have little relevance to life on a British housing estate, but week by week the message is sinking in. The affair between Deirdre and Mike Baldwin on *Coronation Street* may have seemed too trivial to penetrate the consciousness of high-minded individuals but it was not insignificant that it was headline news in the popular press. Books, papers, films, TV, magazines do influence how people react and behave. They establish norms, guidelines which would formerly have been set by the Church or family or local community. If the papers or television pundits say something is OK then they must be right. If a novel or film or soap opera concentrates on the pleasures of illicit sex, and makes light of the pain, their gullible audiences will only discover the reality of broken homes and relationships when it is too late.

Anti-family propaganda

As St Paul warned Timothy there will always be those with 'itching ears' ready to listen, and pursue, some new philosophy, and the past couple of decades have seen no shortage of those. The family is the basis of competitiveness, jealousy, neuroses. We must find a substitute for the family (David Cooper, 1971). Nobody should be expected to remain faithful to one partner for life. We should have 'open' relationships in which we can share our innermost selves, and our bodies. If our partner is jealous that is their problem, not ours (*Marriage and Alternatives*, Libby and Whitehurst, Scott, Foresman and Co., USA, 1977).

Some of these philosophies are well intentioned, earnestly seeking ways to improve conditions. Others deliberately, or inadvertently, undermine relationships and family security.

The influence of the welfare state

In previous centuries families were expected to be responsible for the young, the sick, the elderly, unmarried females and the handicapped. If they did not, or could not, accept that responsibility there was little other provision. The advent of the welfare state brought pension schemes, the National Health Service, State education, social services and social security. There has been much debate whether these provisions have strengthened the family by relieving them of certain burdens and stresses, or undermined it by taking away some of its former functions. Now there is increasing concern as to what will happen when families have those responsibilities thrust back upon them without sufficient resources or back up systems, as seems highly probable.

Future stress
What happens when one of the main reasons for the continuation of the family, the procreation and rearing of children, passes into the hands of the scientists — as it could in the not too distant future? How do we define family in an age when so many households do not conform to the conventional pattern? Is the family the basic unit for the stability of society, and the sanity and security of future generations?

It has already changed drastically in this century. Can it survive the new pressures of the technological revolution? Is there a future for the family?

2

Families 'at risk'

One of the newest Christian magazines has the simple title
Family. I asked its then editor, Anne Townsend, what was
the basic thinking behind the magazine. She replied, 'Marriages in Britain are hurting'. A glance at the contents show
just how far the magazine has moved from the conventional
'pie in the sky'. Christian families are not immune to the
pressures of society in general. Divorce, single-parent
families, teenage traumas and unemployment are affecting
people right across the board.

Inadequate incomes
In some areas the problems are complex and multiple, but
the most obvious presenting need is often financial. 'An inadequate income is one of the most important requirements
for the family' states a discussion paper on families in
Britain (*Happy Families,* Study Commission on the Family,
1980). Yet the rich appear to be staying rich, and the poor
getting rapidly poorer. 'Family poverty remains a major
problem in Britain... exacerbated by growing unemployment and increasing one parent families,' continues the discussion document. A group which campaigns consistently
on behalf of those with low incomes, Child Poverty Action
Group, insists that those most at risk are families with children.

Deterioration of family finances
In terms of taxation and child benefits the position of all
families with children has deteriorated. Child support in
tax paying families is worth less than it was in the 1960s, and
since the Second World War the values of tax allowances for
a single person has risen far more than that for a family with
four children. As far as child benefit is concerned research

shows that the minimum allowance needed for older children in 1982 would have been almost double the actual level.

Effect on the family

Of course it will be argued that people managed in the depression of the thirties, that money does not necessarily bring happiness, but arguments like that invariably come from those with comparatively few financial problems. When each week brings a new struggle to make ends meet a great deal of unhappiness can be generated. Mothers become anxious and irritable. Fathers feel inadequate, children resentful. Marriages break up.

'The man from the council came to look at the damp in our bedrooms', a woman struggling to survive on supplementary benefit explained. 'He said we needed electric fires in the bedroom. I asked him "Who'll pay the bill?". Someone gave me a gas fire instead of the oil heater for the lounge, but they want £29 to fix it.'

She has not got £29. She could not save £29... unless they go without something else. She doesn't smoke. She can't afford alcohol. She doesn't go out... except to her mother's occasionally. She is not a scrounger. She is a decent, sensible woman trying very hard to make a good home for herself and two children in very difficult circumstances.

In such situations Christmas becomes a nightmare. It is more than coincidence that the number of suicides rise with the advent of the season of peace and goodwill. It is no use telling children there is not enough money to buy the delights the 'admen' insist are essential for happy living. They see them in the shops. They can see them in other folk's homes. If their parents cannot afford them they are a failure, as society has already made sure they know, especially if they have committed the unforgivable sin of being unemployed.

Effect of unemployment

Whatever the whitewash brigade may try to kid us, the unemployed are less likely to have a telephone, newspapers, books, washing machines, fridges, holidays or new clothes.

What they are likely to have is poor health, depression, anaemia, and a terrible feeling of rejection and powerlessness.

According to *A Fairer Future for Children* by Mia Kellmer Pringle, published 1980 by Macmillan, 'Families of the long term unemployed have the lowest income, the lowest standard of living and the lowest status of any group of families in the country'. It adds chillingly, 'We have been able to control them socially until now because they have not grasped the irreversible nature of their situation'.

Multiple Problems
Already it is estimated that the number of vulnerable families, or families 'at risk' is as high as 20 per cent. Many of those have multiple problems — finance, housing, unemployment, depression, loneliness, teenage problems. What happens in the next decade, when the present generation of unemployed youngsters become parents, does not bear thinking about... unless you believe in compulsory sterilization.

Violence
Those working with the families most at risk have already suggested that the link between rising unemployment and increasing figures of domestic violence and incest should be urgently researched. In our area, the London borough of Newham, there has been an 11 per cent rise in children on the danger list, and an estimated three to five hundred children die every year in Britain because of abuse. Of these, 5 per cent are the children of parents who may be classified as insane, another 5 per cent have parents who are extremely aggressive, but a staggering 90 per cent are battered and uncared for because of 'inadequate mothering'. This does not mean they are deprived of maternal affection because the mother is going out to work. On the contrary, 83 per cent of the children on the NSPCC 'at risk' register have mothers at home full time. The problems are more likely to come because the parents are very young, isolated,

living in poor housing, unemployed, affected by drink, gambling, debt, didn't want the child in the first place, or the male in the household is not the natural father.

The incidence of battered wives and 'granny bashing' is also highest in conditions of stress, where there are worries about money, homelessness, unemployment or alcoholism. Often the violence is a consequence of violence inflicted during childhood, or a response to intense frustration. It is not pleasant to think of anyone venting their ill feeling on someone weaker or more vulnerable than themselves, yet how many of us can plead guiltless to not lashing out at least verbally when our partner, or children, are not the real cause of our wrath? When fifty parents were asked if they had ever feared they were in danger of losing control of their temper more than half answered 'yes'. Yet the majority came from comfortable, middle class, Christian homes. If they snap under severe strain it should not be difficult to imagine how much quicker breaking point can be reached when the stresses are multiple, or there is no other adult to share the worries.

Isolation
How can a parent cope single-handed with an unemployed teenager who refuses to hand over a portion of his dole money to household expenses? Who do you turn to for advice when you are seventeen, single, and faced with a screaming baby in the middle of the night in a multi-storey block of flats, with the neighbours hammering on the walls?

Isolation is a problem not only for one-parent families, and women at home, but increasingly for the unemployed. There may be people all around but nobody who understands, or appears to care, about your needs. It is only a short step from that frame of mind to the downward spiral of depression, reliance on drugs or alcohol, and attempted suicide.

Dependency
Alcoholism is another problem on the increase. Admissions to hospital have risen by 500 per cent since 1960, and a

growing number are women. The female sex also tends to become dependent on tablets as an escape from difficult situations. In 1975, 12 per cent of British women were taking tranquillizers daily for a period of a month or more each year. Most of these were suffering symptoms associated with the menopause, or were at home with young families.

Self sufficiency?

In such a situation it is hardly realistic to suggest that families should be more self-sufficient, that cuts in social services and the health service will not affect people adversely. They may not impinge too severely on those in employment with private health schemes, insurances, and enough money to educate their children privately. For the unemployed and the underprivileged they can only spell disaster.

However sceptical the more fortunate may be about the value of social services or the volunteer organizations there is no doubt that the plight of many would be a lot harder if their support was not available. When there is no partner, no parent living nearby, and your friends have enough problems of their own, the social worker or the lady from Family Care may be the only people able to offer any future in a seemingly hopeless situation. A nursery place, a week's holiday or a little bit of financial aid can mean all the difference between a family coming through a crisis, or the children being taken into care.

Sharing the problems

There are a terrific number of families who do need guidance and friendship and support; and it need not always be professional. A worker with Family Network, who lives on a large inner city housing estate, believes there is a great need for local lay advisers, someone who understands and appreciates the problems from the inside, who is part of the community, and available to give practical help when the need is most urgent. The growing number of self-help groups have certainly illustrated that those who have experienced a similar problem for themselves may well be able

to share the burden at a far deeper level, and point people
in the direction of the most useful professional help.

In an age of recession and large-scale unemployment the
need will often be practical. What to claim. How to claim it.
Already an estimated £50 million of benefits go unclaimed
every year in London alone. More frequently, or beyond
the 'presenting' problem, the need will be for love, security.
It is a sad reflection on a society which is probing space that
so often we are incapable of reaching the people nearest to
us.

Lack of communication

'Ninety-nine per cent of the phone calls we receive are from
women,' explained a worker co-ordinating our local branch
of Family Network. 'And invariably they complain that they
can't talk to their husbands, or that he won't listen to them.'
The Andy Capps of this world will immediately respond
with some comment about 'nagging wives' but the subject is
far too serious to be brushed flippantly aside. Marriage has
changed. It is no longer an economic contract but a personal relationship. When that relationship flounders, the
whole marriage is put at risk. If the normal response to any
attempt at communication is silence, indifference, or ever
accelerating arguments few people will be content to en-
dure such a state of affairs indefinitely. The fact that the
basis of marriage is seen as companionship, sharing, 'the
best friend I ever had', leaves a great ache in the heart of
those who are unable to achieve such a happy state. Many
marriage counsellors are convinced that marriages are
foundering not because we have lowered our ideals, but because our expectations are too high. As Jack Dominian has
pointed out, 'Our expectations have outstripped our resources. We want a good relationship but lack the skills
needed to understand what is going on in ourselves, and
how to reach through to what is going on in our partner.'

If there is no one to guide, to help us work through these
tensions, families may be rightly described as an 'emotional
pressure cooker'. When extra stresses such as the birth of
the first baby, unemployment, teenage children, the death

of a parent or money worries are added, the situation can become even more explosive.

There is an urgent need for education in relationship skills, and for more counsellors to help couples negotiate the sticky patches every marriage encounters. Otherwise it is all too easy to look for consolation and support from other sources.

Extra-marital relationships
Apparently 40 per cent of women and 60 per cent of men have had an extra-marital affair at some stage. The progressive element may experiment with intimate networks, swinging, and group marriages — but according to the results of a survey reported in the *Guardian* (November 1982) most extra-marital affairs end 'unhappily'.

For the rejected partner there is insecurity, a sense of failure and inadequacy and the basic trust has gone. The other partner can be torn by guilt, and the knowledge of what he or she may be doing to two sets of lives. If we could be taught to channel even half the energy such relationships require back into our marriages maybe we would have fewer frustrated partners complaining 'he/she won't listen' and heading for the divorce courts as the first, or only, option.

3

Divorce, one-parent families and remarriage

According to the National Children's Bureau there has been a 400 per cent increase in the divorce rate over the last twenty years, and it is estimated that one in three marriages now taking place will end in divorce. In 1982 there were 146,698 divorces, involving 158,268 children (OPCS 1982). The cost to the nation in terms of legal aid, childcare, social security payments, etc, has been estimated at a billion pounds a year (NMGC 1983). The cost to the individuals concerned is incalculable. For the partners it brings feelings of guilt, anxiety, rejection, failure, depression, and a terrific sense of bereavement and loss. It also means the division of the home, financial resources, and families. However 'easy' divorce may have become legally, I have met no one who has come through the experience unscathed. Their reaction seems rather to have been 'I wish my partner had died. Death must be easier to cope with than divorce' (see *The Christian and Divorce*, Mowbray, 1981).

Effect on the children
However mature and civilized the adults may try to be, children are torn in two, in decisions over custody and access, and in the confusion of their own feelings. When parents divorce it is as if they are saying to the child 'However much I may say I love you I do not care enough about you to make the effort working at marriage would require of me'.

I know that statement will hurt many who have agonized over their broken marriage and decided that its effects are so destructive they cannot possibly be worse than the effects of divorce. I grieve with them in the agony of that decision, and have nothing but admiration for the effort so many expend to ensure their children suffer as little as possible. From the bitterness of their own experience however I feel sure that many would agree that 'Most children want and need two parents. The regular absence of one is a source of distress, and, however well they adapt — and human beings do adapt to the most challenging situation — the loss is not easy to compensate' (Jack Dominian, *Marriage Faith and Love*, Darton, Longman & Todd, 1981). It can take two years before they begin to stabilize, and the possible long-term effects include neurotic illness, alcoholism, depression, sexual difficulties and anti-social behaviour.

According to a director of the National Council of One-Parent Families, 'The amount which the child suffers as a result of break up depends greatly on the maturity of the parents. If they put their child's interests first, before their own bitterness or hurt, and achieve a reasonable relationship, the children will benefit. If the parents are immature, or bitter, and insecure or use the child as a pawn, the whole situation can be grossly destructive.'

Need of pastoral care
In view of the heartache involved, a group of Catholic women have recently suggested that the Church should exercise more compassion and pastoral care when dealing with broken marriages.

All too often the divorced person is made to feel he has committed the 'unforgivable sin', at a time when he needs all the love and understanding he can get. Of course the Church has a responsibility for discipline. Its major emphasis must inevitably be reconciliation. Christians also need to open their eyes to the world we are living in, and realize that none of us is totally immune to the pressures of the age.

We have no right to 'tut-tut' about other people's broken marriages. We do have an urgent duty to pull out all the stops and do all in our power to affirm marriage, and reduce the suffering of divorce.

Preparation for marriage

Existing preparation and training for marriage is grossly inadequate. Only a small proportion of the people I questioned received any kind of pre-marriage counselling, and most of that was a quick half-hour session with the vicar. It seems ridiculous that people are required to pass a test before they are allowed to drive a car alone, that training for a career can take anything between three to five years, yet we expect couples to make all the transitions, plus responsibility for children, with nothing more than a twenty minute ceremony as proof of their capability.

It is not sufficient to make the excuse that family life is the best and only lasting preparation for a good marriage. It can be a superb grounding. It can also be disastrous. The reality of the situation is that many need to unlearn the patterns they have received from their home life. 'We children had a terrible time with our parents,' explained one teenager. 'They couldn't be in the same room without tearing each other to shreds, physically fighting, or throwing things. Seeing two people like that makes you feel bitter and insecure... not a good picture for family life.' In such situations glib talk about caring, sharing, forgiving, loving is not enough. It needs spelling out in everyday specifics.

Need of a back-up system

Couples need support, counselling, someone they can turn to when the going gets tough. It is now being suggested there should be counselling one year into marriage, or a few months after the ceremony, and that the role of best man could be upgraded. Nobody wants to see people interfering, or organizing other people's marriages, but an improvement in the 'back-up' system is long overdue. The Church is still responsible for a large number of marriages. What is your church doing to ensure those marriages survive? If some of the 'horrific' effects of broken marriages are to be avoided we need to start putting our concern into action. Now.

Divorce — a deviant expression

Fortunately there are some indications of a growing realization that divorce should be a last resort rather than the first option, in that it evades the real issues, and creates as many problems as it solves.

'A picture is beginning to emerge', states Jack Dominian in *Marriage, Faith and Love* (DLT, 1981) 'which indicates that it is indissolubility that reflects most accurately human aspirations and integrity, and that divorce is… a deviant expression. Christianity has the task of convincing society that its opposition to divorce is not mere dogma but a human necessity.'

A minimum commitment

Although it is being suggested that one year's separation should be sufficient ground to prove the irretrievable breakdown of a marriage, there are also moves afoot to make both marriage and divorce more difficult. One idea is that there should be two stages of marriage commitment, one for those with children and another for those without, and that those taking on the responsibility of children should be prepared to commit themselves for a minimum of fifteen years. This works on the basis that marriage may be dissolved but parenthood cannot. Those used to thinking of marriage as a lifelong commitment will probably be horrified by such a suggestion but in America the average length of a marriage is already only seven years.

Need of counsellors

In an imperfect world people do make mistakes. There has to be provision for extreme cases, as Jesus himself recognized. The tragedy is that an awful lot of marriage breakups could be prevented if there were more facilities for counselling and reconciliation. The sad phrase 'if only' drops all too frequently from the lips of the recently divorced. The National Marriage Guidance Council claimed recently that their counsellors are being swamped by the demand for their services. Yet only a tiny proportion of people needing help ever get as far as their doors. The vast majority turn to friends, family, elders and ministers for counsel. Where are the books and training courses to equip people to be better able to cope with this responsibility?

Some enlightened authorities are now beginning to operate conciliation services with the aim of reducing the tensions created by conflicting interests in a divorce, but one of the original aims of the Divorce Reform Act, to point couples to the possibility of reconciliation, seems to be largely ignored. Maybe if Christians began to take the Sermon on the Mount more seriously, and applied themselves to the much needed task of learning to become 'peace-makers' there would be fewer problems in this area.

Single-parent families

There could be a reduction in the number trying to cope as a one-parent family too. According to recent figures (February 1983) one in seven families with children are now headed by a single parent. In inner London the proportion could be as high as one in three. Over 40 per cent of these families will be receiving supplementary benefit, and run the risk of being categorized as scroungers. If they have children and go out to work they will be doubly judged by society. Not only are they single parents they are neglecting their children. It is a 'no win' situation.

Lack of finance is a major problem for single parent families. On average they have to manage on half the income of a two-parent family. The director of the One Parent Families Council has warned that if single-parent families have to continue to struggle in poverty on inadequate benefits growing numbers could end up as no-parent families as the children are taken into care.

Need of understanding and support

Some people are even suggesting that they should no longer be called 'families', as if the loss of a partner, or parent, were not sufficient hardship to bear. Any parent struggling to be father and mother, breadwinner and home-maker, disciplinarian and carer, needs understanding and practical support far more than judgement and discrimination.

Even when there are few problems with housing or money there can still be a terrific sense of isolation. 'Some of the single mums stay to help at playgroup just to be with other people,' said one of the leaders. 'We may be the only adults they chat to all day. It's as much for the mums as the kids.' If the single parent is a father this sense of being 'odd man out' can be even more extreme.

If anyone doubts the hardship of existence as a single parent they need only read some of the literature produced by organizations concerned about their welfare. Gingerbread, Cruse, Child Poverty Action Group, National Council for One-Parent Families, and the new Christian Link Association of Single Parents all understand the problems from the inside, and can often offer practical guidance and support through local self help groups.

Where there is little or no support the adult can easily sink into depression, or a state of nervous exhaustion, particularly if they are coping single handed with the demands of small children or rebellious teenagers. Suicide rates must be just one measure of the stressfulness of the situation:

9.9 per 100,000 of population married
47.9 per 100,000 of population divorced
204.4 per 100,000 of population married and live apart. ie. one-parent families

(Quoted Jack Dominian, *Marriage, Faith and Love*, DLT, 1981.)

Remarriage

Another escape route often attempted is remarriage, or a living-in relationship. Remarriages now make up one-third of all marriages (OPCS 1979) despite all the headaches they can produce. So many problems can be carried over from the first marriage — jealousy, insecurity, problems with the children, fights about money. Maintenance is a particular thorn in the flesh for all concerned. The first wife resents being dependent on the ex-husband, the second wife may find herself in the unenviable position of actually contributing to payments for the first. The male in the middle soon discovers how few men can afford to keep two families. It has been estimated that the breakdown rate for remarriage is as high as 40 per cent, which is higher than that for first marriages. As Jack Dominian comments, 'If first marriages have to be worked at to succeed, second ones need this approach even more' (*Marriage, Faith and Love*).

Step-parenting

For the children remarriage can be even more traumatic than divorce. Step-parents have fallen into the category of wicked witches, ogres and other 'nasties' in the folklore of many countries. Apparently this can be traced to the ambiguity of the relationship. Step-parents have to assume authority and responsibility in the day-to-day running of family affairs yet they have no legal rights as parents. When children can play off parent against parent against step-parent the complications are enormous. One psychologist is quoted as remarking that the feelings caused by step-children do not bear looking at for many people.

With the increase in remarriages the issues raised by step-parenting cannot be ignored, and those coping with tense relationships need the particular love and understanding of the Christian community.

4

Care of the elderly and handicapped

The curtains were closed round a side ward of the maternity unit. The nurses glared at any of the mothers who looked as if they might dare go near. 'What's the matter?' one of the mothers eventually plucked up courage to ask. 'There's something wrong with the baby. It's in the special care unit,' the nurse muttered grimly. The rest of the mothers glanced anxiously at their own babies as if to make certain they were all right. For the rest of their stay they tip-toed past the sideward as if fearful they could catch some dreadful disease. No one saw, or spoke to the 'bereaved' mother. It was easier to pretend such things don't happen.

They do. It is estimated that one child in seven suffers from disability — physical, emotional, intellectual or educational — although the handicaps can include hay fever, asthma, eczema, hare lips and other defects families may not have even categorized as anything other than an irritating peculiarity which seems to affect some families more than others.

Hurtful attitudes
Like colour, handicaps can often be more of a problem for society then for the person or family concerned. Having an adopted black daughter has helped us appreciate the hurt experienced by families with a handicapped child. We have been walking down a street with the toddler beaming in her pushchair, and a person coming in the opposite direction has shuddered and remarked to her companion in a voice obviously intended for us to overhear, 'How can anyone love *that*?'

I have heard people in our local shopping centre comment as they passed a child with Down's Syndrome 'They shouldn't be allowed with normal people'. In such situations it is difficult to know whether to be angry or sorry for the person with such a limited vision. Fortunately I am not a quick thinker and have usually put several blocks behind me before I think of the stinging retort I would like to have made. For the joy and sheer guts of many handicapped children can put so called 'normal' people to shame. How many could cope with the operations, hospital visits, catheters, physiotherapy, special diets, injections, and all the everyday routine of a handicapped person with half their vigour and determination?

Special care
That is not to deny the extra burden of care borne by the families of handicapped children. Special boots, dressings, exercises all take time. Doors, beds, bathrooms, cars may require special modifications. Money, energy and time may be in short supply. The other children in the family can suffer. Caring for a severely handicapped child is a long-term, costly commitment.

Cause for concern
Those faced with the appalling options presented by abortion, and modern medical practices stand in special need of all the love, prayer and practical support those surrounding them can muster. They will continue to need it if that child is allowed to survive, as they come to terms with their own grief, and society's attitudes. They will still need it when the 'child' is forty, and telling the butcher for the tenth time that it is her birthday.

They do not want pity, or to be treated like lepers. They are ordinary families with a practical problem. They need time off, holidays, knowledge of help lines, baby-sitters, someone to talk to, someone to care. Those needs could become more urgent if the cutbacks in the social and health services continue.

Concern for the elderly

So could the dilemmas facing the families of elderly people. 'Honour your father and mother' is one of the basic tenets of Christianity. How do you apply that in practical terms when that parent is frail, lonely, two hundred miles away, and there is neither space nor sufficient emotional resources to absorb him or her into the normal three bedroomed semi, vibrating with teenagers, their music and their traumas? 'I dread to think' is a fairly typical response from those already beginning to face this tension.

'We just live one day at a time, and do our best as situations arise,' explained one woman where health problems are already a major difficulty for her ageing parents. Will such philosophies be sufficient to see us through a future situation in which there will be increasing numbers of elderly? The number of over-65s has increased by one-third in the last twenty years, and numbers of very aged are increasing at a rapid rate. With half of all hospital beds and 35 per cent of the Health and Personal Social Services budget being allocated to the over-65s it is easy to see why the Government are desperately trying to shift the burden of care back on to the family.

What about the carers?

But have the family ever really abdicated that responsibility? Recent research indicates that it is a lie that families no longer care. 'Significant numbers' of elderly people are cared for by their families. Estimates suggest that more women are looking after elderly people than under-16s, and three out of four women, and four out of five men over eighty-five are likely to live with their relatives. When it is realized that only 32 per cent of the over-85s have no disability this burden of care can become considerable. If the 'carer' is single and struggling to hold down a job the tensions are obvious. If they remain at home, unaided, the frustrations can soon build up to fever pitch. Married women can find themselves torn between the conflicting demands of parents, children and husband... to say nothing of their own needs.

Absorbing an elderly relative into a family unit is not always the best answer. Far from accommodating a frail old lady content to knit quietly in the corner many families have found themselves taken over by a powerful matriarch who dominates decisions and destroys relationships. I can think of at least eight instances where the presence of an elderly mother either has, or could, seriously damage that family. When there are children involved there are differences in attitudes, values, priorities, and practice between three generations, to say nothing of differences in personalities. It takes the patience of Job and the fortitude of a saint to balance that kind of combination.

The cost of commitment

Confinement to bed, incontinence, loss of memory and general cantankerousness are just a few of the problems carers may have to face. 'At least with young children there is some light at the end of the tunnel,' explained a nurse who has just given up her job in a geriatric hospital because it is too tough. 'If they're refractory you can spank them or send them to bed, and you know one day they will become less dependent.'

Full-time carers of the elderly do not even have the release of 'going off duty' or the company of other nurses to help them laugh off tense situations. A superb television play, *Where's the key?*, highlighted how the statutory agencies are reluctant to share responsibility, if only for a short term, unless the caretaker, or the family, are actually snapping under the strain. 'I want practical help, not pills,' the distracted daughter wailed at her GP. That cry must be echoed from every street in our land.

If one person has to assume the burden of care fifty-two weeks of the year it will not be long before their own health suffers. Bad backs, constant depression, nerves and over-tiredness are just a few of the symptoms.

Abuse of the elderly

When the provocation or pressures are extreme, fatigue and resentment may spill over into violence. At the moment

there is little documentary evidence available but it has been
suggested that one in ten old people may be 'at risk'.
'Granny bashing' is not confined to the underprivileged sections of society either. In most instances there has been no
previous violence, and the relationship was initially loving.
Stress, isolation, and increasing disability have soured the
relationship. A typical abuser is a middle-aged woman
suffering from nerves.

Support schemes
It should not be difficult to see how essential it is that anyone caring for an infirm old person should have some form
of relief regularly. Something as simple as offering to
granny-sit for an hour or two could mean all the difference
in the world to a carer trapped between four walls twenty-
four hours a day.

   If families are to be enabled to care for their old people,
there must be some provision for 'time out' occasionally. We
need more schemes like the one in Leeds where 'foster'
families are paid to care for the elderly parent while their
own family has a much needed break. Another interesting
initiative is the self help group, the Association of Carers,
where those caring for an elderly person can meet for a
chat, a cup of tea, and the reassurance they are not alone…
however much they may feel it. The book *You Alone Care* by
Heather McKenzie (SPCK, 1980) also contains sound practical advice, particularly about the emotional hazards of caring for elderly parents.

Living alone
Old people living alone are a common cause of concern for
their families, who may feel responsible, but powerless to do
anything about it. Are they keeping themselves warm?
What will they do about shopping when the weather is bad?
What if they are ill, or have an accident, or get attacked?
How can they survive when they have nothing but the television and the cat for company? But how much of this guilt
is misplaced? One-third of old people do live alone, have no
incapacity, and want their independence. Most studies

show that elderly parents prefer not to live with their children. They like to be near, but not too near, and letters, phone calls, and visits, especially continuing contact with the grand-children are all greatly appreciated.

The most vulnerable are those with no children, or male children alone, for the largest amount of help given to elderly people comes from women. It is women too who invariably staff the lunch clubs, meals on wheels, home help services and good neighbour schemes which mean so much to the isolated elderly.

Support networks

How adequately they cope depends to a large extent on the strength of their support networks. Those connected with some form of group, whether it is a club, association, or church fellowship, remain optimistic and express satisfaction with their lifestyle. Isolation is an enormous problem in modern society, and the person prepared to sit and chat, and listen to the anecdotes is exercising a much needed ministry. Neighbours and friends can also provide information and advice about welfare benefits and services. Over one-third of pensioners are not claiming supplementary benefit to which they are entitled. Leaflets in post offices, libraries, and Citizens Advice Bureaux give information on rent rebates, rate rebates, heating allowances, attendance allowances, etc. But the forms and red tape may be daunting and old people particularly resistant to 'living off the State'. It needs emphasizing continually that the payments are not charity but the responsibility of a caring society and their right.

Valuable contribution

Another myth which needs debunking in a society which increasingly equates work with worth is the idea that retirement means the end of purposeful existence. A wealth of experience, expertise and wisdom has been accumulated by the older generation. Projects such as the Help the Aged Side by Side Programme are doing much to release some of the skills and first-hand knowledge which are otherwise lying untapped.

'Our daughter did a project in school on the Second World War,' a parent explained. 'We didn't think the children would be at all interested, but it went like wildfire. The teacher was inundated with photographs, mementoes and accounts of events from grannies and grandads.'

Often too it is the grans and grandads who provide the prams, hand-knitted garments and gifts of money to help young couples struggling to establish their own family unit. They are also still the prime source of child care. In the USSR and China grandmothers have been the enabling factor in the employment of young married women, and in our own society grandmothers often have more time for the grandchildren than their hard-pressed mothers. Our son's close relationship with his grandparents is largely due to the fact that they had him for a whole day each week when he was small — which was a source of great satisfaction and benefit for all concerned.

Voluntary work

Our senior citizens' contribution to voluntary work is also invaluable. Anyone regarding retirement as a one-way ticket to premature senility would do well to read such positive books as John Cansdale's *The Bonus Years* (Paternoster, 1979) and *The Christian in Retirement* by William Purcell (Mowbray, 1982). People are individuals with potential for growth, and a positive contribution to offer — whatever their age or circumstances, but health, education and finance are all important factors in determining the quality of life for the elderly. The jet-setting grandmother bears little comparison with her fragile counterpart confined to a cot in the geriatric ward.

Future planning

As the numbers of elderly people increase, costs are going to rise astronomically. According to the study document *Families in Focus*, 'The need for help and support for elderly people will rise sharply in the next two decades.' Yet when someone tried to raise the subject at a recent Christian conference she was told it was too personal for general discussion.

If euthanasia is not to be the first or only option offered to the elderly in the very near future we need a change in attitudes, and urgent research — NOW. With the number of women in paid employment, and the complexity of relationships resulting from divorce and remarriage it can no longer be assumed that women are willing or able to assume the entire burden of responsibility for the elderly. As life expectancy increases, sixty year olds may be found caring for parents in their eighties.

Should carers be expected to cope unaided, or should we be thinking more in terms of partnership? Could there be more co-operation between the State, Church, voluntary organizations, and the families concerned? If we know now that the 'position of elderly people in our society will be one of the major challenges for social policy for the remainder of the century' (*Families in Focus*, Study Commission on the Family, 1981) what provisions do we need to make in terms of housing, health services, relief care and leisure facilities? How aware are we of existing needs and opportunities for service amongst the elderly in our community? A Sunday lunch organized by a group of local churches to discuss the family attracted a high proportion of elderly people. Why? A plateful of bangers and mash and one miserable gas fire in an enormous hall was apparently more attractive in company with other people than the loneliness of their own homes.

Sheltered accommodation
No doubt a number of those present were struggling to maintain full-sized houses with all the attendant bills for rates, maintenance and heating. While organizations such as Age Concern and Help the Aged insist that old people should have the choice to retain their independence, it seems sad that the choices have to be so extreme. Old people want their independence. Their children worry themselves sick if they are on their own. What can we do to encourage more initiatives in sheltered housing?

Certain areas of Birmingham are adapting tower blocks for the elderly — complete with warden, intercoms, community rooms and security systems. Some churches are releasing land and premises to housing associations with special provision to nominate a certain number of tenancies. A vicar in Kent has suggested a mobile home could be airlifted into the garden to accommodate grandmother, or other elderly relatives.

There are no simple answers, but can we afford to ignore such an important subject? The care of the weak, the elderly, the underprivileged has always been a requisite for the family of God. How are we going to respond to that challenge?

5

Women and work

'It's the women going out to work that's causing all the trouble,' grumbled an elderly gent during a discussion on the family. As usual there was a chorus of agreement. Working women are frequently the scapegoats for unemployment, marriage break-up and juvenile delinquency.

'There is no doubt that the employment of women, and particularly mothers, outside the home is one of the most significant social changes affecting family life,' states the discussion document *Families in Focus* (SCF, 1981). But are these changes necessarily for the worse? Are working women the real root of all the ills of which they are accused? Is there so much 'Christian' concern now because it is a phenomenon relatively new to the middle classes, and Christian males are only just beginning to realize how threatened their territory/power base is becoming?

A significant proportion of working class wives have always worked — or at least drifted in and out of the labour market as pregnancies, or part-time work, permitted. Often they had no alternative — compelled by inadequate wages, and too many mouths to feed. My mother, mother-in-law and grandmother all worked — in offices, shops, factories, or private houses — at whatever presented itself and was not too destructive of family patterns.

Family economy
In pre-industrial times women were indispensable to the family-based industries. In agricultural areas women were responsible for the dairy, poultry, pigs, orchards and gardens. They helped in the harvesting. They spun and wove. If their husbands were craftsmen they were responsible for preparing and finishing their work. Women produced

most of the beer and bread in the retail trade. They also produced and reared the next generation of workers and in many ways were the cornerstone of the family economy. It has even been suggested that work and food would have been their first priority, and that children had 'minimal claim' on material resources and their parents' time. Women not contributing to the family economy would have been regarded as 'lazy' and anathema to the writer of Proverbs whose 'virtuous' lady is extolled for her industry, business acumen, and administrative skills; an early model of a typical working wife (Proverbs 31). It is hard to imagine what he would have made of the leisured middle-class lady produced by the industrial revolution.

Division of work and home
As small family industries were replaced by large-scale factories and mills, demanding full-time specialized skills, numbers of women in the labour force declined. Married women returned to work mainly in times of crisis and poverty, and the working wife became a sign of need. Female skills and energy became concentrated on managing domestic affairs, and there was an increasing emphasis on children and childcare.

Reserve labour force
In recent decades women have been regarded as a reserve labour force, to be encouraged, or discouraged, from working according to the demands of industry and commerce. During the two world wars and the expansion of the fifties, women were actively encouraged to participate in the drive for productivity. In tougher times they are blamed for taking men's jobs, despite the fact that most women are working in the lower paid light manufacturing and service industries.

Influence of education
Today, we have the ridiculous situation where women are educated and indoctrinated with the entire 'You must use your brains and abilities to the fullest extent' philosophy,

then expected to take meekly to motherhood and domesticity without so much as a backward glance. When they become depressed by the limitations and frustrations of a job for which they have had little or no preparation, they are labelled 'neurotic' or inadequate. If they return to paid employment once the children are past the crucial early years they are regarded as selfish and materialistic.

Economics

In fact the main reason married women return to work is economic, but not for the 'pin money' of popular mythology. Of families with the youngest child under five, 40 per cent have incomes near or below the level of supplementary benefit, and over two million women are the breadwinners in their household. Many say they would prefer to stay at home but can't afford to, and one million work to provide the basic standard of living, rent, rates, bread, heating, clothes. There would be four times as many families facing poverty if their mothers did not work.

If there is to be a return to 'family values' someone is going to have to do some long hard thinking about the financial aspects. Between 1948 and 1980 pensions increased twenty-one times, Child benefit increased nine times. On the other hand tax for a childless couple has risen by 122 per cent, that for a two child family has soared an astronomical 382 per cent. State child support is worth less today, relative to average earnings, than when the family allowances were introduced after the war. It is hardly fair to blame women for returning to paid employment when government policies make it very hard for them to remain at home. The work ethic is too deeply inbred into the working population for many mothers to sit idly twiddling their fingers when the children need new shoes or coats, and there is not sufficient money available. For many sections of the population, especially the West Indian community, being a good mother includes being an economic provider.

Use of skills

Even when there are fewer financial pressures women may

still feel guilty that they are not using the skills and talents they have been trained to develop. Many of these skills are invaluable in childcare, and the organization and administration of a household, but many others may have to be suppressed, or go unacknowledged in the loneliness of our nuclear household set up.

Isolation

Whether they live in tower blocks or charming suburban estates, isolation remains a major problem for women at home, especially young women more accustomed to the bustle and companionship of the office or shop. As a social worker remarked when she was relating the problems of a young mum with a new baby, 'I'd feel nobody cared if I didn't see anybody all day.'

However many alternatives some sections of the community may invent for themselves, work still remains the main meeting place for many people in our society. There are lunch breaks, tea breaks, people to chat to as you pass their desk or machine. Men may joke about their women gossiping over the fence, or in the supermarket, but they find social isolation is no joke when they are faced with retirement or redundancy.

Low status

Along with the loss of their mates, leaving paid employment also involves a lowering in status. Our work-orientated society values people in terms of what they do, rather than what they are. Housework is regarded as one of the most menial tasks — far beneath the dignity of the average male. When asked what they do, most women not in paid employment reply apologetically 'Oh, I'm just a housewife'. Often that is the end of the conversation. When I say I am a writer or a teacher I can see my value rising at least ten points in the other person's estimation. In her study *Housewife* (Pelican, 1976) Ann Oakley points out that 'A phonetic reduction of the term housewife produces the appellation "hussy". "Hussy" means "worthless woman".'

Little reward

How many other sections of society would be content to work double the normal working hours, with no holidays or weekends off, in a job which is more monotonous, fragmented and socially isolated than factory work for little or no reward. I have actually heard one woman begging her husband for pocket money on a day out, and a local MP describe child benefit as the woman's income. I know that a large number of men have no more spending money than their wives by the time the bills are paid, but at least they feel as if they have received some reward for their labours when they collect their wage packets. Women have no increments, promotion prospects or other ways of knowing that their job is of value. Is it any wonder that they get steamed up if their family forget the one day it is customary to tell mothers their work is appreciated? If their more usual response is to criticize the lumpy custard, or complain that a shirt has gone pink in the wash, and there is no attempt to praise an enjoyable meal or the umpteen times the clothes emerge ironed and laundered unscathed, can they complain when mum finds a new sense of identity and worth with her return to work?

Dissatisfaction

Ann Oakley discovered that 70 per cent of housewives expressed dissatisfaction with housework, and in a *Woman's Own* poll four out of five said they would want to work even if there were no financial pressures. The fact that the vast majority are employed in low paid, semi or unskilled jobs shows just how low housework must rank in comparison.

'There are aspects of the housewife role that make it almost impossible for a woman of adult intelligence to retain a sense of human identity, the firm core of self, or I without which a human being, man or woman, is not truly alive,' wrote Betty Friedan in *The Feminine Mystique* (Penguin, 1965).

'Amen' echo a large number of frustrated females the length and breadth of the country, especially those struggling to juggle the two conflicting demands of a house and children.

Incompatible roles
How can you reconcile a child's needs to experiment, imitate, question, use up their boundless supply of energy,
and have your total, undivided attention with such 'petty'
details as cooking, washing, shopping, and keeping a house
clean and tidy? The housewife role is simply not compatible
with that of mother — especially in the child's early years.
They walk over newly washed floors, splodge sticky fingers
over walls, spill things, wet things, and leave a trail of toys
and clothes in their wake. They can undo what you have
done in a fraction of the time it took you to do it. If you are
so foolish as to think you can snatch a few minutes for yourself, reading or studying or watching television, they have
an enormous variety of diversionary tactics. They interrupt
conversations. They demand drinks, games, toilet, anything to attract attention — including trimming the cat's
whiskers, or cutting the telephone lead.

On my fortieth birthday a friend teased '21 today'. 'You
must be joking,' I retorted. 'I wouldn't want that again. All
those tough years when the children were small. It's much
more comfortable being forty,' despite the fact that those
toddlers are now teenagers. Yet I am trained to work with
children. I have always worked with them — in school,
Sunday school, holiday clubs, youth groups, residential
nurseries. I like children... other people's children. I joke
that it's easier to cope with thirty children in school all day
than my own four at home. I can guarantee that within five
minutes of being inside the house the fur will be flying and
my nerves in shreds. Why? My kids are no worse (or better)
than anyone else's. I am no more neurotic than the next
mum.

Conflicting needs
Maybe the answer lies in our closeness to our children, the
way they reflect our own faults and failures; the fact that we
can't hand them over at the end of the day, that so often
their needs do conflict with our own, especially when it
comes to women and work.

'How can you have a relationship with your children if

you're working all day,' a local mum grieved. 'It's no use if you just feed them and shove them into bed each night.' Neither is it always beneficial for a mother to be home, totally absorbed in her children twenty-four hours a day. Is it not possible somehow, to achieve a balance?

Part-time work

For whatever their critics may say, women are working. An EEC Labour Force survey in 1979 put the figure at 40 per cent of all married women, and over half of the mainly Christian women I questioned were working. Many of these move in and out of the economy as circumstances dictate, the typical pattern being to work at the beginning of the marriage (69.6 per cent), drop out when the children are young, return gradually after the important pre-school years (27.9 per cent after six years), until 59.7 per cent are working again after twenty-four years (1971 census). Of these the vast majority are employed on a part-time basis, and many more would prefer to work part-time if the work was available.

Future predictions

Unless it proves impossible most intend to continue in employment. In a *Daily Mirror* survey in 1979 only 15 per cent of mothers said they had no intention of ever working. Reasons that might make wives consider abandoning paid employment are major crises, such as illness, redundancy, too much stress, and a negative effect on self or the family. Even then a large number say they would be unhappy, or feel restricted or frustrated, or worry about money. In a survey in *Options* magazine (May 1982) most women admitted that they felt frustrated at home with small children, but they felt their presence at home was essential. They wanted to enjoy their babies, but were nearly unanimous that they would return to work when their children were at school. One mother summed up a general feeling that 'Every human being must be themselves at sometime or another — not just someone's mother. I lost my identity, and work gave it back.'

Benefits of work

Many studies are coming to a similar conclusion, that work has a benign or positive effect on women. Certainly the women in my own extensive circle of acquaintances seem to thrive on combining two careers. I don't know any working mums who have 'gone under' permanently or seriously, although they may suffer temporary setbacks, or flashes of panic and guilt. Without making too much effort I can think of at least three intelligent, articulate women needing medical assistance for 'depression' when they were confined to the role of housewife. Those who are working say they enjoy their work, find it stimulating, like using their skills, and get a sense of personal fulfilment. They feel they are better for it — more interesting, refreshed, happier. They are no longer just the chief cook and bottle washer, and wives and husbands said it was beneficial in reducing money worries and frustrations.

'Work provided a fuller life, the type of stimulus I needed,' said one mum. 'As I thrived on it so did the family. It prevented me being a mother hen, and I had no time to brood over my decrepit body.'

Worries about the children

Work may well have a positive effect for women but what about the effect it has on children? Childcare experts have consistently decreed that children need emotional security and attention, besides the basic physical requirements of food, warmth and shelter. Traditionally the majority of the population are likely to think in terms of childcare being the prerogative of women — or rather one woman — the mother. Women produce the children. They should also be responsible for rearing them, runs the argument.

Yet many are beginning to question whether there has been an over-emphasis on one person bearing full responsibility. In non-industrial societies the mother is supported by the family, and the wider community. In their study *Working Couples* (Routledge & Kegan Paul, 1978) Rapoport and Rapoport state 'Mothers in most societies are expected to spend 4-6 hours each day outside the homestead.' In the

Asian communities of our larger cities mothers still spend a
large proportion of their day working (either inside or outside the home) and grandparents and older brothers and
sisters assume responsibility for the younger members of
the family.

Of course there are dangers of women becoming over-
burdened and overtired but are they any greater than the
dangers for a mother confined to home and children with
no support from friends or family, including her husband?
Rapoport and Rapoport conclude that above the level of
child abuse it is difficult to find differences and that most
children are very adaptable. One startling figure that would
seem to turn the usual 'mother at home's best' theory
abruptly on its head however is the fact that 83 per cent of
the children on the NSPCC 'at risk' register have mothers at
home full-time.

Substitute care

Another factor which determines the child's ability to adapt
is the mother's personality, and the quality of substitute care
and supervision. If the parents are happy with their work
and childcare arrangements, and the substitute parent is
stable and responsive the children thrive. Unfortunately
quality care costs and is not always easy to obtain.

For a start there are never sufficient nurseries to meet
demands. In a *Woman's Own* survey two-thirds of the
women wanted properly equipped, staffed nurseries. Only
one in twenty had a place. There are over 30,000 child-
minders registered for 92,000 children, although estimates
suggest the number actually being cared for is nearer
330,000. Many of these minders are doing a superb job for
very low pay, but despite the efforts of local authorities and
the National Childminding Association there is still concern
that too many children are left in situations where they
receive little stimulation or emotional support.

At the other end of the scale children may be cared for by
the home help, nanny, au pair or boarding school, whose
capability and consistency can vary as greatly as any child-
minders. Lack of consistency seems to be the major prob-

lem, for the children who suffer most are the ones subjected
to a series of different care arrangements. The most reliable
care appears to come, as it has always done, from the family.
In the *Woman's Own* survey fathers were responsible for 64
per cent of the substitute care, and more serious studies
have also concluded that a 'very high proportion' of childcare is provided by the family or neighbours. It has also
been suggested that working-class children receive more
parental care than a hundred years ago.

Patterns of work
Nevertheless there is still a strong instinctive belief that
small children need their mothers around, and that mum
should be there to welcome the child on its return from
school. Less than one in four under-fives have working
mums, and both husband and wife are happier if the
mother with pre-school children can remain at home. The
proportion of women going out to work increases with the
age of their children. A typical pattern for a working wife
seems to be remaining at home until the children go to
school, followed by part-time work, with any overlap
covered by husband or family or friends.

Help or hindrance?
Women themselves will hotly dispute any suggestion that
their children suffer because of their work, with the excep-
tion of those who have to work long hours or have inadequate substitute care. Work is seen as helping the family
rather than escaping from it, and the children of well-
organized working mums are often more independent and
mature than their more cossetted counterparts. The
National Children's Bureau reports that there is little detri-
mental evidence against working mothers, and some positive. Their income may make a 'crucial contribution' to the
family's living standards, and results of several studies have
'not been such to support the fear that mothers at work are
guilty of any lack of responsibility towards their children'
(Ronald Fletcher, *The Family and Marriage in Britain*, Penguin, 1973, 3rd edition).

Delinquency

In contrast to this, 'how much children see of their fathers has a crucial and long lasting effect on them' (*Kitchen Sink, or Swim*, Deirdre Sanders with Jane Reed, Penguin, 1982), and juvenile delinquency, which is usually blamed on working mothers, is more likely to be the result of inadequate fathering. Of juvenile offenders, 98 per cent are without fathers, or father subbstitutes, and a study in Britain revealed that delinquent boys see greater defects in their father's role than in their mother's.

Limited Autonomy

This does not mean that there are no risks involved in women going out to work but that on the whole mothers are likely to be aware of the dangers and try to minimize, or compensate for them. Some women work because they have learnt from experience that they do not take easily to life at home, and that it is better for everyone if they are working. Mothers of one-parent families may have little choice. Others know instinctively that they could not balance a full-time job and a family, and opt for part-time employment. The number of women working full-time has hardly changed in twenty years, but the proportion working part-time has nearly trebled.

In other words women want fulfilment and autonomy, but not at the expense of their small children. For the vast majority of women the welfare of their children is paramount, and most are prepared to accept the restrictions placed upon them by young children, and their husband's career. In some cases this has included opting out of paid employment if it is creating more problems than it solves in terms of income tax, loss of rebates, travelling expenses, substitute care, household reorganization, etc. One mother described feeling as though she was being 'pulled apart by two demands' and not doing credit to teaching or motherhood. The family had to have first priority, even if it meant managing on less money. Sometimes it is the children who exhibit the first signals all is not well. Nightmares, aggressive or withdrawn children, clingy, tired, tear-

ful children are all danger signs which may indicate something is amiss.

Tiredness

Tiredness is one of the main disadvantages of trying to combine work and running a home too. 'There is always too
much to do, leading on to tiredness and irritation,' is a typical complaint, although many know they would fill their day
with as much busy-ness to help them survive if they did not
go out to work. A doctor writing in the *Lancet* described the
symptoms of a worn-out mother as nervous tension, irritability, severe headaches and indigestion. He diagnosed the
two main causes as callous husbands and inconsiderate
employers.

Short cutting

Wives at home usually have more time but less money, so
their housekeeping and cooking tends to be more elabor-
ate. Wives in paid employment have more money but less
time so they rely more on gadgets, paid help and streamlin-
ing jobs. Much scorn has been poured on books such as
Shirley Conran's *Superwoman*, but holding two jobs in
balance does require organization, and the ability to sort out
priorities. Non-iron materials, convenience foods, super-
markets with drive-in car parks, and endless lists are the
stock in trade of the working wife. Survival often depends
on the ability to disregard inessential tasks, or to keep them
to a minimum. In our household nobody seems to mind
that dusting has a very low priority, and the vacuum cleaner
only makes an appearance once or twice a week. The pressure comes when women who make a fetish of housework
are about to pay a visit. It's only then I really become aware
of the pawmarks on the window, and the cobweb hanging
elegantly from the lampshade. It has become a standing
joke now that when my mother says she would like to spend
a fortnight with us we know she isn't thinking in terms of
sitting in the garden in a deckchair. We survive by compromise, and an acceptance of one another's different
priorities and personalities — usually. For if working

women are to avoid the ever-present danger of overload
they have to know their own capabilities, and limitations,
and stick within that framework, whatever other people
may say or think.

Co-operation
They also need proper co-operation from the rest of the
family. 'I never put my job first, but the family have to
realize that the job affects my performance in the home,'
said one working mum. 'Otherwise I feel martyred.' Many
women working at home, or outside the home, would identify with that feeling, and would envy the family a young
adult described as a working team. In that household jobs
were done by whoever was least under pressure, following
many years of patient groundwork and a good working
model from the adult male.

Overload
The more usual norm seems to be a grudging acceptance
that mum should work, providing it doesn't make any difference to the smooth running of the family. In other
words, 'as long as I don't have to do anything to help.' It
seems to make little difference if that second income is
essential to family finances. In fact the burden on working-
class women is likely to be greater in that often they are
more houseproud and probably have to work longer hours.
    'Some days I haven't even sat down to have lunch,' be-
wailed one mum with a young toddler. 'I can understand
that men are tired at the end of a hard day, that they want to
put their feet up, and collapse behind a paper, as long as
they appreciate that we do too.'

Unequal division of labour
The crux of the problem seems to be that old patterns die
hard. Men still want to cling to the old image of the little
woman at home ready to attend to their every need, regardless of the hours she is already expending in paid, or unpaid, labour. Whatever people may say about the value of
childcare and homecare the message that is still coming

through loud and clear to the female population is
'Women's work is nothing. Any idiot could do it. My work is
far more important. Don't expect me to do yours.' Drying a
few dishes does not rectify the distinct, and often unequal,
division of labour. Research shows that working wives still
undertake the bulk of the housework, and although there is
some move towards sharing it is not compatible with the
wife's extra work.

Is this just? Equitable? Right? Is it any wonder women
feel resentful? Why should one member of the partnership
regard household chores as 'helping' and expect lavish
praise for his efforts, while the other's contribution goes un-
noticed, if not actually subverted, day after day?

Lack of appreciation
One of my favourite stories is that of the husband who
vacuumed the house while his wife was out. On her return
he sat waiting for some acknowledgement. He waited and
waited. At last he could contain himself no longer. 'Didn't
you notice I'd done the vacuum cleaning?' he asked. 'Yes,'
his wife replied patiently. 'It's terrible being taken for
granted, isn't it.' No one is asking for the smooth talking, or
red roses, so often advocated by the glossy magazines. What
is needed is a change of attitude, a realization that woman's
contribution is of value, even if in cash terms their reward
may be non-existent.

The contribution women make to the family, and national
economy, in terms of unpaid domestic and childcare service
is immense. Their emotional investment in the family is incalculable. Yet when it is suggested there should be some
form of pay for mothercare, women are accused of being
mercenary, and there is immediate outcry. How else are
they to know that their work is of value — especially if the
family value it so much they consider it beneath their dignity to contribute, and believe that they have every right to
grumble, destroy, or create extra work at will. Men rightly
fear the trade union women create for themselves wherever
they gather, for a simmering sense of injustice about pay
and conditions of service is never far beneath the surface.

So often we 'get by' on the old assumptions without really stopping to assess work loads, emotional pressures, and ability to cope in difficult situations, particularly the isolating monotony of working at home.

Change in attitude
Change is difficult. Nobody knows that more than women. Part of the ambivalence experienced by them is the result of the two tensions tearing them apart — their biological urge to nurture, care, home-make, and the desire for personal fulfilment and development which is partly the result of education, and partly to do with the use of talents, creativity, the need to grow which is inbuilt into the special creatures, male and female, made in the image of God. Their male partners have an equally tough battle to fight; the instincts, attitudes, prejudices, expectations, which are adding unnecessarily to this conflict. It is understandable that men do not want increased responsibility or work load in the home, but conditions have changed. Women have changed.

Increased independence
However much men may dislike it, women are more independent. In an *Options* survey 63 per cent of the women thought they could earn enough to live comfortably without their partner, and the State does provide some form of safety net for those unable to earn.

It is not surprising that a great deal of concern is now being expressed for the marriage relationship once the wife returns to work, for the adjustments to be made by both husband and wife are enormous. After years of isolation and feeling of little worth, women returning to work are delighted to discover that they actually do have some value, status, identity. Life no longer has to revolve around the children or the house. If the husband doesn't like it, tough luck. He's had several years of servitude and sacrifice. Now it's someone else's turn. Problems. How many men can cope with the change in lifestyle and priorities that it is likely to produce? It would be interesting to know how many mid-life crises are related to the male's inability to cope with his female's sudden, and long overdue, assertion of independence. It would also be fascinating to discover if men turn to younger women because of their youthful sexuality or simply for more malleable material to remould in the expected role of docile domestic.

Superiority or service?
St Paul and the Church Fathers have a lot to answer for in confirming men in their inbuilt tendency towards dominance, aggression, and superiority. How does this fit with Jesus' upturning of the world's values? If he had married, would he have thumped in from work demanding a cup of tea and subdued silence from the rest of the family while he recovered his equanimity? Would he have regarded child-minding as beneath him, or would he have been down on the floor busy with the building bricks? We know from the New Testament that he cooked fish, washed feet, made sure there was sufficient bread for the multitude, and wine for the wedding. He cared about the sick, the young, the outcasts; qualities and behaviour traditionally more associated with women. When Martha was bustling around expressing resentment at her sister's apparent lack of concern for household affairs, he didn't condemn Mary for failing in her female role, but told Martha to sort out her priorities.

There is a tendency in some circles to talk about sacrifice and service as if they are specially feminine virtues. Is this right? Is there one gospel for men and another for women? If the male population consider housework and childcare too menial and time-consuming doesn't that give them any understanding of the effect it can have on their wives? Does scripture really support the strict division of labour and role some preachers imply is essential for salvation, or at least for acceptance in some sections of the Christian community? Are these ideas necessarily Christian, or more to do with tradition and social structure?

Dual commitment
Time and again in scripture women and men are reminded

of their responsibility towards one another, and their children. The marriage service is a public statement of belief in
the value of family life and relationships. Can women and
children really be blamed for feeling resentful if the male of
the household then appears to have more commitment to
his career, or the Church, or the numerous activities and
involvements that can crowd out the ones upon whom he
should be having the greatest influence? If the father abdi-
cates his role, should he really be surprised to discover he
has little, or no, authority or relationship with his teenage
children? The childcare expert, Dr Spock, says that it will be
a 'great day' when fathers realize that the care of their
children is as important as their jobs and careers. Various
studies show that fathers becoming more involved in
childcare is beneficial for the children, and the fathers.
Husbands may say they need reassurance from their working wives that their first loyalty is to the family. Women
need exactly the same kind of reassurance from their
husbands.

In an era when women do work, there is a need to balance
the requirements of the whole family — mothers, fathers
and children. How that balance is achieved depends to a
large extent on the priorities, personalities and background
of the individual family.

Dual careers
One version is the dual career family; where both parents
are working and the children are cared for by neighbours,
grandparents, nursery care, etc. This may, or may not, be
accompanied by a sharing of roles. Available data suggests
that in 10-20 per cent of households where both parents are
working childcare is shared, but the wife is still largely
responsible for organizing, planning and performing
household tasks.

Job sharing
With the decrease in the number of jobs available, and an
increased concern about the involvement of fathers in
childcare, some couples are opting for job sharing. If one

job is shared between two people there will be less money coming into the household, but fewer hours spent on work and more time available for home and family.

Although the prospect of spending more hours with their partner may not be every couple's image of wedded bliss, researchers assure us that it can minimize conflict by making both partners more aware of the realities of the other person's situation. In Norway there has been a programme to propagate work sharing studies (1971, Norway's Family Council) and such patterns are seen as the 'only way that working couples can manage without a level of stress which erodes the gains from being a working couple' (Norwegian study, *Working Couples*, Rapoport and Rapoport).

Role reversal

A minority of couples (under 5 per cent) are working on a principle of role reversal, where the woman goes out to work, and the male takes over responsibility for childcare, and to a more limited degree, the running of the household. 'I wouldn't have had children if my partner had not been willing to share responsibility,' explained a highly intelligent woman in a top administrative position. 'I knew I was not suited for childcare all the time, and would be bored, ratty and resentful if I had to stay at home. When our first baby was born we learnt how to put on nappies etc, together. It might not come easy to a man, but what makes them think it is easy for a woman? My husband is good at cooking, but it does mean that the house is a tip at times. Our standards are not the same. He doesn't feel emasculated by the situation, and can cope with clinic, playgroups etc, with confidence, though it would be tough for lots of men. He has a great interest, involvement in politics, so it's not a true role reversal. It must be very hard for the unemployed, stuck at home, dependent, isolated, with no money. We are in a very privileged position.

So far there are no signs of disturbance in the children (3 and 1 year). They're quite happy when I leave, and have a closer relationship with dad. If I became exhausted, or they were ill and needed me, I would have to consider changing the pattern. At the moment the main problem seems to be in other people's minds. At parties when they ask "What does your husband do?" and I say "nothing" they think he's either unemployed or has a private income. And how do you fill in forms which demand occupation. Househusband doesn't sound right. I think most of the critics are insecure. They're unsure of their own position.'

However convinced the partners may be about their choice, it should not be lightly undertaken. It is not easy running counter to biological and sociological conditioning, and there are many pitfalls to be avoided.

Communal living
Experiments in communal living have also often resulted in the discovery that people are bound by human limitations and inclinations. The most famous, the kibbutzim in Israel, are now beginning to switch back to parents being more involved in childcare, and the bulk of female work is still in the domestic sector. In most communes women are still involved in traditional female tasks, and some Christian communities have become so extreme men are not even allowed in the kitchen to make a cup of coffee or to help dry the dishes.

There may be new initiatives in communal housing, and community networks of childcare, but most people are still of the opinion that parents should be the chief minders of children, and it seems highly unlikely that there will be any large-scale takeover of household and childcaring tasks in western society.

Pay for mothercare
In fact it may be that many women are working who would actually prefer to remain at home. A survey in an inner city area in 1979 revealed that 75 per cent of women believed that 'real fulfilment' came from home and childcare rather than a job. Suggestions that women should be paid wages for housework, or mothercare, or some form of 'responsibility allowance' as in France and Hungary, are

likely to receive strong opposition from many quarters, but could relieve some of the financial pressures to go out to work.

Attitude of society

I know it will be argued that women should perform their duties out of love, that they should expect to make sacrifices for their family, but women, like the unemployed, will continue to believe they are as valuable as society, and their family, tells them. It is no use blaming women's liberation for degrading/devaluing housework and childcare. The problem is much more basic, and widespread. 'I made a conscious decision not to go out to work,' said a vicar's wife with a young child. 'And still, from the bishop downwards, people ask "When are you going back to work?" It doesn't seem to matter that I do at least half a dozen unpaid jobs.'

A creative task

In face of that kind of opposition it is hard to believe those who try to redress the balance by insisting that the role of housewife and mother is one of the most fulfilling, demanding and creative jobs the bulk of the female population will ever undertake. It doesn't feel as if you are doing a creative job if the toddler has been sick all over the bed, the washing machine has emptied suds over the kitchen floor, and the only sensible conversation you have had all day has been with the cat. If women are to be encouraged to choose not to work the option has to be attractive and realistic.

Future predictions

At the moment women appear to be voting with their feet. All indications point to an increase in the number of working couples in the future. This does not mean wholesale abandonment of infants, or toddlers screaming desperately for their mothers, but the traditional pattern of mother at home while the children are young, followed by a return to work as the children become more independent.

A constant temptation
This immediately presents problems for young families. In
a consumer orientated society it is tempting to envy older
couples with a double income, and forget that they too
once had to forfeit an evening out in favour of a new pair
of shoes for the four-year-old. The unequal distribution of
wealth is no excuse for neglecting to weigh the advantages
and disadvantages of a wife returning to paid employment.

Unsupervised children
According to official estimates 20 per cent of five- to ten-
year-olds are left alone during school holidays, and 15 per
cent after school. This lack of supervision can lead to traffic
accidents, delinquent behaviour, and accidents in the
home. More than a quarter of the burns cases admitted to
hospital involve unsupervised children. One positive
response to this has been the setting up of latchkey schemes,
and holiday playschemes, which provide activities for children out of school hours. These may be based on school
premises, church halls, community centres or private
houses, and are staffed by paid and voluntary workers.
    This can appear as 'dumping' children, shelving respon-
sibility, but for the working mum with no real option about
the hours she works they can spell salvation, a safe environment for the children, and a terrific easing of the burden of
worry and guilt. There has been greater demand for after
school and holiday care than for care for the under-fives for
nearly two decades, which could open up another bridge
into the community for those seeking ways of 'reaching
through' to the needs of their area.

Sickness
Another point of stress is childcare during sickness.
Although I have found little research material about this it
does seem that if there is no reliable substitute care available women simply take time off work, and illness is certainly seen as one of the main reasons women would give
up work.

Added stress
Recent research has revealed another factor to be taken into consideration. An increasing number of women are becoming victims of industrial stress, and needing tranquillizers to cope. Although it may be argued that a fair number also need tranquillizers to cope at home, the extra pressures on women doing two jobs are obvious. Often to obtain the job they have to be better than their male counterparts, and despite equality of opportunity, need to be twice as good to get promotion. Yet because of their family commitments they are less free to travel, or stay late, and are likely to be torn by anxiety if something is amiss at home.

Lack of time
Another trend causing concern is the number of women copying the bad habits of the male population, and putting work as their first priority. However well organized the home may be, children do still need their parents, to listen, to do things with them, to give them their time. Colour television, continental holidays, video games and the latest fashions are no real substitutes for a mum and dad working all hours. The materialistic philosophies underlying present day society present a terrific challenge to the Christian community. If we really believe that spiritual/emotional security is more important than possessions how are we communicating that to a world with a very different value system?

Weighing priorities
How do we sort out our own priorities? Do we constantly bring them under the judgement of God, or are they moulded more by what the people around us are doing, or our own inclination? Powerful forces are at work, both openly and surreptitiously. Opinions can be manipulated by the media, political powers, and religious leaders. Are we driven about by every wind that blows, or do we assess, evaluate, pray and make our decisions responsibly and realistically? Then do we allow for the fact that others may

have different priorities and come to a different decision?

Freedom of choice
'I cannot say that I have been particularly good at being a mother of small children,' explained one of my friends. 'Depression, anxiety about money, social isolation and consequent short-temperedness have been my lot. Whatever is said about working mothers it certainly was the answer for us.' By contrast another gave up a good career when she was pregnant because she thought it best to 'do one job well'. She finds motherhood the most 'complex and rewarding job anyone could have' and has no desire to return to paid employment because being a housewife is a full-time job. A third works part-time. 'It doesn't pay to do more than a certain amount of work,' she explained, 'by the time I've paid bus fares, baby minder, income tax, and we lose our rate rebate. We could use some extra money, but it's not worth it in terms of stress on my husband and child. It might be OK if we had a gran round the corner, but he's too young for nursery.' Providing parents can assess their circumstances and personalities as clearly as those three women, there is hope for the future. French research shows that it is not what parents do, but how they do it. 'Children want their parents to be happy, to feel personally fulfilled and not guilty, martyred or trapped, in either their domestic or occupational roles', Rapoport and Rapoport conclude in their study *Working Couples*.

Guilt
There are always plenty of people around ready to point the finger of blame, and guilt can be equally destructive for the mother at home thinking she is not contributing sufficiently and the mother going out to work who is made to feel she is failing her children and husband. If women have sorted out their priorities properly, and nobody is suffering adversely as a result of their activities, maybe they should start leaving the guilt with those who may have little appreciation of the factors that have led to their decision.

Hope for the future

Whatever the critics may say, the track records of women show that in spite of the unequal burden of housework (on average a working wife does twenty-six hours, the husband thirty-six minutes per week) women are not only coping with being both married and employed, they are actually happier. The ones who seem to be having most difficulty in adjusting are the men, particularly Christian men. There is still an expectation around that at marriage women should trade all their previous training and talents for a life of domestic servitude.

Fortunately, apart from a small minority who still see a distinct division between men and women's work, the younger generation do appear to be thinking more in terms of sharing, equality, partnership, working as a team. As one commented, 'We all make the place dirty. Why not help clear it up. It's always worked in our house.' They still have one big proviso, however, that mum should be at home when the children are young, even if the family needs the money.

Need for negotiation

Whichever way work and family patterns develop in the future there will be times when the interests of men, women and children are in conflict. There will be tensions to sort out, feelings of resentment and frustration to face and rectify, misunderstandings to set right. Women will need to understand the stresses of employment, and un-employment. Husbands will need to realize how much their family needs them.

New initiatives

If some of the explosive issues revolving round the subject of women and work are to be defused, we need new initiatives to deal with the situation. Employers could reduce tensions over holidays and illness with more flexible working hours. Women at home could be greatly helped by 'adopted mums' or grans prepared to get alongside them and befriend them, to reduce the sense of isolation, and inevitable tensions that arise from learning to parent. There could be more emphasis on the importance and creativity of parenthood, including financial incentives and some system of credits, acknowledging the skills and maturity gained during that experience. Fathers could be encouraged to take more part in family life. Children could be better prepared for marriage and parenthood — in school and in the home.

If people really believe that 'Bringing up a family is a social and economic function, and every bit as important as any contribution made to business and industry, commerce or the professions' (*Parenting in the eighties*, Parenting Papers 2, National Children's Bureau, 1982), it will need more than smooth talking or ranting from the pulpit to persuade the female population that this conclusion comes from conviction and experience and is not just another plot to keep woman firmly 'in her place'.

6

The influence of feminism

'In the beginning God said, "Let us make man in our own image, in the likeness of ourselves..." and God created man in the image of himself, in the image of God he created him, male and female he created them.' (Gen.1. 26-27, Jerusalem Bible). So far, so good. Two beings, in God's image, created by God, equal in value in his sight. Now read on. 'Yahweh God said, "It is not good that the man soil Yahweh God fashioned all the wild beasts and all the birds of heaven but no helpmate suitable for man was found for him. So Yahweh God made the man fall into a deep sleep. And while he slept, he took one of the ribs and enclosed it in flesh. Yahweh God built the rib he had taken from the man into a woman, and brought her to the man. The man exclaimed, "This at last is bone from my bones, and flesh from my flesh: This is to be called woman, for this was taken from man." This is why a man leaves his father and mother and joins himself to his wife, and they become one body.' (Gen. 2.18-24, Jerusalem Bible).

Problems. Is this an image of a superb relationship, a working together of two different, but complementary beings, mutually dependent, needing one another? Or does the 'spare rib' bit imply that woman was just an afterthought, something inferior, second best? And how do you interpret the word 'helpmate'? Does it mean some kind of support system, essential to the smooth running of the fragile male ego? Or should it be interpreted as companion, partner, 'a power equal to', as an American theologian is now suggesting?

Power or partnership?

Questions such as these have disturbed the Church for
centuries, and are at the root of a great deal of controversy
surrounding male/female relationships today. Should
marriage be for companionship, sharing, friendship, joint
responsibility, as so many couples believe? Or should the
male be superior, the more dominant partner, whatever
combination of personalities and circumstances make up
the marriage? Are the present day 'daughters of Eve'
challenging only male traditions and interpretations of
scripture in their insistence on equality of worth, or are
they defying the divine initiative and laying themselves
open to the condemnation of both man and God?

Passing the buck

The story of the Fall has raised similar problems. Generations of priests, theologians and artists have presented Eve
as the seductress, tempting man to his downfall. Was this
really the intention of the story, or should it be viewed as
an illustration of how we all make mistakes, and then try to
shift the blame onto someone else's shoulders, instead of
facing up to our own responsibility? Rather than allocating
degrees of blame, wouldn't we do better to stick to the New
Testament. 'Everyone has sinned and is far away from
God's saving presence' (Rom. 3.23, Good News). And even
if woman was responsible for the fall of mankind from
grace, isn't that countermanded by our redemption in
Jesus? As Paul reminds us, 'For just as all people die because of their union with Adam [Note, Adam, not Eve], in
the same way all will be raised to life because of their union
with Christ' (I Cor. 15.22). However many times we pass
the buck one thing is certain, the curse imposed on Eve is
not easily removed. Modern techniques may have gone
some way to easing the pain of childbirth, but women are
still struggling against the domination of men.

Second class citizenship

As early as the books of Leviticus and Deuteronomy we
have records of how women were legally, socially and

emotionally subject to men. They were 'bought' in marriage, could be divorced for 'any reason whatsoever' and had little freedom. In the temple and the synagogue they were restricted to certain parts, and were classified as 'impure' as a result of menstruation and childbearing. They could be stoned to death for adultery, while the male population indulged their fancies in a seemingly endless array of slaves, concubines and polygamous marriages. They received little education, other than initiation into domestic and agricultural tasks expected as their contribution to a nomadic community where work was necessary for survival. In such circumstances it is hardly surprising Jewish boys were taught to thank God daily that they were not born a woman.

This inequality was not confined to the Jewish community either. Throughout the ancient world women were held in low esteem, classed alongside children, slaves and imbeciles. Women were dependent beings, relying first on their father, and then their husband. If they had no male to support them, like Ruth and Naomi, they were objects of pity, whose shame could only be removed by another male.

Exceptions to the rule
Despite these restrictions, the Old Testament has several stories of strong, independent female personalities. There is Esther who defied a king and saved her nation, Deborah the prophet, and the women who were instrumental in rescuing Moses from the clutches of Pharaoh.

But it took Jesus, the Son of God, to give women their true value in society. Like his dealings with the lepers, his attitude to women was revolutionary. He allowed the woman with the issue of blood to touch him. He discussed theology with the Samaritan woman. He told Mary she had chosen the 'better thing' when she sat listening to his discourses instead of assisting Martha with the housework. Women were drawn to him because he treated them like no man had ever treated them before, with respect. Dorothy L. Sayers summarizes this superbly. In an essay entitled 'Are

Women Human' (*Unpopular Opinions*, Gollancz 1947), she states, 'Perhaps it is no wonder that the women were first at the Cradle and last at the Cross. They had never known a man like this Man — a prophet and teacher who never nagged at them, never flattered or coaxed or patronized, who never made arch jokes about them... who rebuked without querulousness and praised without condescension; who took their questions and arguments seriously; who never mapped out their sphere for them, never urged them to be feminine or jeered at them for being female, who had no axe to grind and no uneasy male dignity to defend; who took them as he found them and was completely unself-conscious. There is no act, no sermon, no parable in the whole Gospel that borrows its pungency from female perversity; nobody could possibly guess from the words and deeds of Jesus that there was anything "funny" about woman's nature.'

Women may not have been disciples in the sense that the twelve were, but they were certainly amongst his followers ministering to his needs, and supporting him financially. Despite their lack of training in the scriptures they were quick to recognize his divinity, and were amongst the first to witness to the resurrection.

Women in the early Church
This new sense of freedom and worth seems to have persisted into the early Church. Women were full members. They were baptized, and helped found churches and prayer meetings. Lydia was a founder member of the church at Philippi. Priscilla was a teacher and leader, Phoebe is described as a deaconess. There seems to have been a special order of widows responsible for giving instruction to younger women, and women were accepted as prophets and evangelists. In fact women played a 'considerable part' in the missionary work, worship and teaching of the early Church.

Paul's attitude to women
It may be this very reason that led to the restrictions Paul

appears to place upon women in the epistles. Was Paul a woman hater, as could be concluded from some of his statements, or was he reacting to situations where the Church could have fallen into disrepute because the position of women in the Church was so far ahead of contemporary society? Were his instructions binding for all times, or guidelines for young churches in a specific situation?

Women or men, chattering, arguing, babbling in tongues would be a distraction in any assembly, and in the ancient world a woman with an uncovered head was the sign of a temple prostitute. Paul was a child of his times, bound by his upbringing and social convention. In his society women were subordinate and some of his instructions reflect those attitudes.

At other times his ideas seem closer to those of his master. The exhortation 'Husbands, love your wives just as Christ loved the church and gave his life for it.' (Eph. 5.25) must have raised more than a few eyebrows in a society where male needs would normally have been the first consideration.

Such teaching still has power to transform relationships when it is put into effect. In Africa, where men are traditionally the head of the household, making all the decisions and expecting obedience from their womenfolk, when Christ becomes the head of a household the couple are far more likely to work things through together. It is easy to criticize Paul for going back on some of the freedom made possible in Jesus, without fully appreciating the reaction he probably received to some of his teaching. 'There is no difference between Jews and Gentiles, slaves and free men, between men and women; you are all one in union with Christ Jesus' (Gal. 3.28, Good News Bible) was hardly likely to have been any more popular in the early Church than it is in a society which is still divided by barriers of race, class and sex.

Attitude of the Church Fathers

Clinging to the familiar, the known, is always more attractive than stepping out into uncharted territory, and although there appear to have been women ministers and deaconesses at the beginning of the second century, the office of presbyteress was disbanded by the Council of Laodicea three hundred years after the death of Jesus.

It seems likely, says George Tavard in *Women in Christian Tradition* (Notre Dame, London, 1973) 'that the final status of women in the church proceeded from a reaction against the fear of scandal — from acquiescence to social conventions rather than from theological principles'. It is also highly possible that the two extreme reactions to women perpetrated by the celibate Church Fathers are a direct result of their own fear of the power of sexual instincts. One tradition sees women as inferior, cursed, the temptress, the other regards Mary as the ideal woman and puts on all women this image of perfection. This schizophrenia seems to have blighted Christian thinking ever since.

Much of Western Christian thinking was influenced by Augustine, who produced such gems as the idea that the soul entered man on the fortieth day after conception, but didn't enter woman until the eightieth day. Like many others he equated woman with flesh, the man with spirit.

Difference of opinion
Such attitudes largely went unchallenged until women began to receive some form of education, and were more able to question male authority and assumptions. By the late Middle Ages it was reluctantly accepted that woman might be equal spiritually, but not biologically. Prominent leaders such as John Knox and Calvin were amongst those who believed that women were for childrearing, and men. They were cursed by the sin of Eve, and because they were made from a rib they were crooked and crafty.

One sane voice in the wilderness seems to have been the Quaker, George Fox, who wrote in 1698 'For man and woman were helpmates in the image of God, and in righteousness and holiness in the dominion before they fell, but after the Fall, in the Transgression, the Man was made to rule over his wife, but in the restoration by Christ, into the image of God and his righteousness — they are helps meet,

Man and Woman, as they were before the Fall.' (*Not in God's Image*, Virago, 1979, ed. Julia O'Faolain and Lauro Martines).

Present day attitudes

Oh for such enlightenment in the post women's lib era, for whether it is a reaction to feminism, or the old instinctive desire for dominance there is increasing pressure from certain sections that women should conform to a subservient role. Women may be regarded as equal in business, law, medicine, politics, society in general, but a large number of Christian males still expect their women to be dependent, submissive, secondary. In the Brethren Church the women are supposed to remain silent, and to keep their heads covered. In the Anglican Church they have come to the conclusion that the arguments against women priests are more psychological and sociological than theological, yet ordination is postponed on the grounds that the time is not yet ripe. In all branches of the Church the women are assigned to tasks such as flower arranging, cleaning, sick visiting, helping in the Sunday school, but not anything involving control or authority, such as preaching or administering Holy Communion, despite the fact that women form the overwhelming majority of most congregations.

Female reactions

'Women are not seeking power but they do want to alleviate their powerlessness, want to serve,' reported the Laity Commission survey 1977-80. They decided women want partnership and participation, rather than paternalism. 'When we are no longer driven by powerlessness to excessive need for power we can express our human potency in many ways,' wrote Betty Friedan in *The Second Stage* (Michael Joseph). 'Human sex, human politics, the creative further reaches of the human spirit.'

It seems nothing less than tragic that more often women are pushed into the reverse experience. Feelings of hurt, anger, frustration and low self-esteem bind and destroy them. Gifts are ignored, or under-used. Church language is riddled with male images, father, son, brothers, man. In some circles there is pressure to conform to a stereotype of womanhood, and services such as the churching of women have done nothing to improve their sense of worth.

Despite the gospel emphasis on the value of the individual this 'good news' seems slow in penetrating church circles. In a 1973 questionnaire (Newman Association Family Committee) 85 per cent felt there was discrimination against women in the Church, and 90 per cent felt that such discrimination was incompatible with the justice demanded by Jesus. For centuries the Church has preached the doctrine of male superiority, and as religion is seen as an 'important shaper and enforcer of women's image and role in culture and society' (*Dispossessed Daughters of Eve*, Susan Dowell & Linda Hurcombe, SCM, 1981) it is not really surprising that it has come under attack.

The birth of feminism

Chief among its critics are those concerned for women's rights. Contrary to popular opinion this is not just the by-product of the twentieth century. The fight for equality dates back to the eighteenth century, and one tradition is strongly linked to the social and moral reforms associated with evangelical Christianity. The belief in individual conversion went hand in hand with an acceptance of the need for self-realization, freedom and autonomy. Often women were seen not just as equal to men, but in many ways superior. Men were held largely responsible for the plight of prostitutes, the ruin of families through alcoholism, and the sexual exploitation of black women. Concern about such issues led to a move out of the home and into politics, although traditional roles were rarely questioned. It was more a matter of bringing domestic values to bear on public issues, and conservative rather than radical.

The exclusion of women from the anti-slavery convention in 1840 was followed by the Seneca Falls Convention in 1848, at which most of the speakers were women, many of them Quakers. They protested against half the human race being denied the right to become fully human, and this is seen as the beginning of feminism as an organized social movement.

Equal rights

A second strand of the feminist movement concentrated on equal rights. As early as 1792 Mary Wollstonecraft had written *A Vindication of the Rights of Women*, which argued for emancipation, and declared the belief in female independence and equality. The American Revolution with its Declaration of Independence was one of the main inspirations for the feminist belief that men and women are created equal. In his essay on the 'Subjection of Women' John Stuart Mills compared the power of husbands to that of a despot, or slave owner. By the 1860s votes for women had become a dominant theme, and there was pressure for reform of the legal position of married women, particularly as far as custody, property and earnings were concerned. The education of women was another vital issue in an age where opinions were divided between the need for education equal with men, and education for the domestic role.

The socialist tradition

The third strand of the movement was biased more towards the socialist tradition. They looked for an equal share in organization, and co-operation more than competition. There were various experiments in communal living. These were intended to emancipate women rather than abolish the family, but many were short-lived, the practice proving far more difficult than the theory. Practical assistance in the shape of birth control, day nurseries and easier access to abortion were intended to make life easier for working class women.

The years between 1897 and 1920 are regarded by many as the Golden Years, with the vote finally being won in 1928. In the United Kingdom this was followed by four decades of social reform, the welfare state being largely attributed to welfare feminism and the Labour Party. Marriage and family life were still seen as the basis of the welfare state how-

ever, and the depression and aftermath of two world wars
(including the baby boom) ensured that there was no move
away from traditional values and attitudes.

The feminine mystique

On the contrary. Women appear to have become totally absorbed in the 'feminine mystique', the image of woman as
healthy, beautiful, home-, child- and husband-centred, as
perpetrated by the magazines and advertisers. It was not
until the 1960s that the situation began to change. A manpower shortage in Britain and America led politicians and
employers actively to encourage women to return to work.
Before long women were campaigning for equal pay, equal
opportunities and equal status. In America the National
Organisation of women grew from one thousand members
in 1967 to forty thousand in 1974.

At the same time rumbles of discontent and disenchantment began to emerge from various quarters about the
emptiness of the housewife role. Critics of Women's Liberation blame the movement for stirring unrest. Those inside
would claim that the reaction was spontaneous, growing out
of a corporate awareness of unease and imprisonment.
Betty Friedan's book *The Feminine Mystique*, published in
America in 1963, is described as the classic text of the
modern women's movement. In it she describes the di-
lemma of educated women confined to the housewife role.
The sense of irritability, emptiness, incompleteness, of having no existence of one's own is first defined as the 'problem
that has no name' and later identified as a problem of identity. The need to grow and fulfil our own potential is a basic
human need. Betty Friedan articulated a common feeling;
the role of housewife does not allow such growth, and is at
the root of female restlessness and frustration.

Women's Liberation

Women's Liberation has been interpreted and distorted in
various ways, the most usual stereotype being that of anti-
man, anti-family, bra-burning fanatics. Certainly radicals
like Shulamith Firestone see women's oppression as the

result of reproduction with no real answer being possible until children can be produced independently of the female body. They believe that when this happens the family will no longer need to exist as it has been known. Women and children will be able to create their own families, with the help of state aid and childcare alternatives. The mother-child relationship is often idealized but men may be regarded as no more than temporary sexual partners. Women are quite able to survive without them, gaining more from the friendship and sisterhood of other women. Marriage is seen as patriarchal, based on male authority and female dependency. The search for alternatives includes group marriages, free love, celibacy, and lesbianism.

Not all women concerned for female rights would take such extreme positions, however. As its name implies the women's liberation movement is made up of a variety of groups rather than a main organization. As in the Church emphases vary according to the individuals who make up each group, but there is a central belief in equality and free-dom for women. Most are against women being used as sex objects, and the double standard which allows men sexual licence. They want their sexuality under their own control instead of being defined and limited by men. Although it is not pleasant reading, the novel *The Woman's Room* by Marilyn French portrays the kind of experiences which have led to such reactions. Betty Friedan summarizes women's libbers not as men haters, but as women who want to grow, discern, live freely, use their ability and have the right to education, a career and the vote.

Feminism
The Fontana Dictionary of Modern Thought defines feminism as 'Advocacy of rights and equality of women in social, economic and political spheres, a commitment to the funda-mental alteration of women's role in society'. It is concerned with defining areas of oppression and creating structures for growth and justice.

Shift in the balance of power

Traditionally women have been dependent, limited by their biological make-up to the rearing and nurturing of children. Men have been seen as aggressive, the hunters, the breadwinners, relying more on their physical strength. Various social changes have led to a shift in this pattern. Contraception has meant fewer children. There have been more gadgets to cut down the amount of time needing to be spent on housework. Men are no longer the sole breadwinners. More job opportunities for women, and the safety net of the welfare state, have given women more financial independence. The relaxation of the divorce laws and a new sense of their own worth as individuals has produced a reduction in the tolerance level of attitudes and behaviour that women are prepared to accept.

Through all levels of society women are making their protest felt. The more articulate argue about stereotypes, identity and biological and sociological conditioning. The women in more downtown areas continue to work all hours, cook the Sunday lunch, wait for their male to return from the pub, put up his feet and snooze off the effects of his meal and the liquid refreshment, till the day something snaps and he gets his dinner in his lap, or the door slammed in his face.

Women's role in society is a key factor in male/female relationship. It has changed. It could change even more radically with the technological and social upheaval we find ourselves facing. Women no longer find their sole identity in marriage and the family. Rather the reverse. Many actually find their identity being destroyed by it. Jessie Bernard, professor of sociology and author of the book *The Future of Marriage*, concluded that marriage can be a poor deal for women.

Equality or enmity

Men have experienced their problems too, with the adjustments required by the change in the balance of power. Women might want equality not enmity but Betty Friedan foresaw that there would be trouble during the transition

period while couples negotiated what that meant in practice. At the moment opinion seems divided between those
who fear and avoid the issues, those who rush into full-scale
confrontation, and a third group who realize it will create
conflict, but that there is no way round if they and their
marriage are to flourish and grow. We can only hope that
Betty Friedan was correct when she predicted that ulti-
mately both sexes would benefit.

Submission or self determination?
Since the recession and unemployment of the seventies
there has been a decline in more radical attitudes, and a split
between the moderates and the radicals in the feminist
movement. In her latest book, *The Second Stage* (Michael
Joseph, 1982), Betty Friedan reminds her followers that the
founder members of NOW all had families. She sees a new
'problem with no name' emerging, that of living with equality, and reconciling freedom with the need for love, children, family and home. But the suggestion that women need
to recognize the centrality of the family in their lives, and
press for new kinds of family rather than denial of the
family, was not well received by the more radical elements.
At the other extreme submission is a strong message being
preached by some American evangelists. A visitor to the
American Bible belt of California said the position of
women there had hardly changed since the witches of
Salem.

   Should we all breathe a sigh of relief, and pray for a rapid
return to the 'old order', or do women (and men) have too
much to lose from a return to their previous state? Is the
healthy woman the one who is conscious of being a person
who just happens to be a woman, or the one with so little
sense of self worth she must conform to a certain role? Is it
unChristian to challenge assumptions and ask for freedom
to make choices, including the terrible choice about abortion?

Scriptural principles
Was Paul reaffirming a principle that we break at our peril

when he taught that the husband should be head of the wife? Or was he bringing human judgement and tradition to bear on a relationship intended to be one of partnership when human sin and frailty do not intervene? Should men be envied or pitied if they have to accept ultimate responsibility for their family unit? Can there be democracy in marriage, or only the extremes of anarchy or tyranny? Is it crying for the moon to dream of a time 'When women and men can look at each other and see what is good in the other sex (and) learn to be themselves without fear of each other'. (Una Kroll, *Flesh of my Flesh*, Darton, Longman & Todd, 1975)? Is feminism an invention of the devil as some truly believe, or part of the search for freedom and justice which those who follow in the footsteps of one of the greatest freedom fighters will find hard to ignore?

An important issue

There are so many issues involved, so many relationships at stake, the subject cannot be shoved under the carpet and forgotten, unless all women are given a lobotomy at birth. Research has proved that they are not inferior academically. They can read, listen to radio and TV documentaries, talk to other women, at work, at the school gate, in groups. They are questioning, is this right? Is it just? Is it good, for me, my partner, my family? How do I prepare my children for future upheavals? For, as Shulamith Firestone and many prophets of the future foresee, when the genetic engineers remove reproduction away from the human body we face even more adjustments in our thinking. The male population may yearn nostalgically for a return to the era of the sweet, passive, dependent female. The future reality may be more like that expressed by a twelve-year-old venting her frustration about male attitudes encountered at home and at school. 'I'm never going to get married. No man's going to boss me around.'

Is it mere coincidence that the women first pressing for female emancipation were also involved in the anti-slavery campaigns? It would be interesting to know how much of their motivation was social conscience, and how much identification? One definition of emancipation is being led out of a state of slavery, and sexism is described as any 'Attitude, action or institutional structure which systematically subordinates a person or group on grounds of sex' (Una Kroll, *Flesh of my Flesh*).

When it comes to sexism the critics can certainly have a field day in the Church. They do not have to look far for male images of God, male language in worship, male priests, male heroes, male interpreters of the Bible, masculine authority in the home, and church. It has been too much for some women who have found the liberation Christ offers bound up in male structures and interpretation. They have moved into mysticism, pantheism, witchcraft, anything that gets them away from the oppression they have experienced in the Church.

Feminist theology

Over the last thirty years there has also been an interest in feminist theology. This challenges the male perspective of Christianity and seeks to make Christianity more accessible to those who have been turned off by the male, white, western interpretation of it.

In *Dispossessed Daughters of Eve* the authors state 'The overwhelming task of feminist theology is... to face the fact that Christian theology is guilty of sexism (as it has been guilty of racism and classism) but also to affirm that this faith, this theology is not irredeemably sexist. This is a critical mission within all organized religion... not to substitute but to reclaim history, restoring a balance, creating a more just, and life loving world.'

This means asking questions, challenging assumptions, searching for truth. At a conference in London in 1983 Rosemary Radford Ruether led a session on the subject of women, men and power. Groups worked on topics such as power and service in the gospels, women in church history, women's writing, man-made language, and love and power in relationships between women and men.

Local groups of Christian feminists have a diverse membership and approach but some form of centralization through organizations such as Christian Women's Information and Resources. Most are small and attempt to be non-hierarchical in structure. Subjects at meetings range through equal rights, forms of worship, sexuality, family life, authority, economics and the new theology.

Nearly a hundred years ago Elizabeth Cady Stanton wrote a 'Woman's Bible' in which she suggested that woman was actually superior to man in that she at least argued with the serpent, whereas Adam meekly followed her suggestions. More recent attempts to emphasize the feminine side of God, and give more prominence to the Foremothers of Christianity are greeted with just as much hostility, scepticism and ridicule as she received. It appears that traditional scholarship is slow to respond to the challenge thrown out by feminist theology.

'We searched diligently but were unable to discover any traditional opponent to the women's movement in the Church who were actually conversant with the questions raised by feminist theologians,' report Susan Dowell and Linda Hurcombe in *Dispossessed Daughters of Eve*. As with attitudes to race and hanging, many feel that there has often been a selective use of scripture to prove points rather than a general over-view of the Bible, and a testing of attitudes against the behaviour and teaching of Jesus.

Ostriches or eagles?

'I always felt Jesus was the only male who understood me,' bewailed a young Catholic woman in a magazine article. She was expressing the feeling of a number of women equally hurt and bewildered by male attitudes in a male-dominated Church. From Dorothy L. Sayers onwards women have not argued with Jesus. The gospel is about freedom and wholeness, which is exactly what feminists are seeking. The arguments are rather with the organized Church, which is seen as twisting the basic principles and oppressing any search for justice. It is as if women are being told there is one law for men, and another for women. You must stick to your role, your place, regardless of the talents and ability the Creator has given you, and your individual circumstances.

Such views are strongly opposed by many Christian feminists who agree that 'A return to that sound reformation principle of the priesthood of all believers is long overdue' (*Dispossessed Daughters of Eve*). Of course women have responsibilities to their families, but that is not their only, or entire, contribution to society. They no longer need to spend a large proportion of their lives turning a mangle, baking bread, or heating the copper. Modern technology and contraception have enormously reduced the amount of time and energy needed to be expended on the home. Men, and children, resent the cluckings of a mother hen trying to justify her existence by centring her life on their interests and activities. But they seem equally reluctant to allow women to 'stretch their wings and fly like an eagle' (Radio 4 documentary). If God pours out his spirit indiscriminately on male and female he must be enormously frustrated when that incredibly liberating power is quenched and dampened by resistance to anything different or unconventional, especially when people are being hindered from coming to a knowledge of him because of the hurtful attitudes they encounter.

Male liberation
The question now being asked is not so much how we can liberate women from men, but how can we achieve liberation for men, especially Christian men? Can they be freed from attitudes and lifestyles which are destructive? How can they be helped through the insecurities which make them feel so threatened by women's liberation, or any other challenge to male supremacy? Will they lose out and lose face if they start to share power, or could they discover real authority?

Skills and characteristics which have previously been thought of as 'feminine' are now the ones being favoured in patterns of management. Similarly the number of men 'at risk' from heart disease and other fatal illnesses in the 45-60 age bracket must make them seriously question their priorities and lifestyle, even if they choose to ignore the warnings from their womenfolk. New attitudes to work and family could maybe restore men to their children, and to themselves and their partners.

In America a 'wave of men' are already opting out of promotions which involve disturbing their families, and many companies are finding great difficulty in getting and keeping executives. A survey in 1979 found that men from the most oppressed backgrounds still had money and getting ahead as their main concern, but that the majority valued personal growth, self fulfilment, love and family life more than making money and getting ahead.

Facing up to feelings

'The reason why women run rings around men is that men couldn't pass an 'O' level in describing their own feelings. That is why they are so violent — it's the only way they can articulate their passions while denying the importance of them,' wrote Philip Hodson, who describes himself as Britain's only male agony columnist. If men are to be liberated from such responses it will be a long hard haul as women have already found in their own search for identity. The ability to live with oneself involves insight into your own personality — its strengths and its weaknesses, which is never an easy journey, particularly if your female counterpart appears to be travelling in the opposite direction.

Change in attitudes

There may be more changes in legislation with men joining in with claims for paternity leave and childcare allowances, as in Sweden. But the real battles are being fought in everyday relationships, in the need to change attitudes even more than laws. 'Fight for your right on your own shop floor,' suggested an amusing magazine article. 'Parity begins at home.'

On the surface the arguments may be about who cleans out the gerbil, or polishes the car. The real conflicts go much deeper. They are to do with respect, the value we ascribe to the other person; the right/freedom we allow them to be a person. Leaving a trail of dirty socks and underwear over the bedroom floor may appear a trivial matter to a hard-pressed business executive or a teenager

struggling with examinations. To the woman of the house
they say far more clearly than words just how much value
the family places upon her.

A generation in conflict

Any number of books and articles have been written on the
theme of Superwoman; how to organize, administrate, gain
co-operation in the business of running a home, and in the
world of paid employment. Whether women really want
this double burden, and the headaches it can create if the
male becomes financially dependent, is debatable.

On the other hand they are just as likely to reject the
image of the 'earth mother' totally absorbed in home and
family. Women are a 'generation in conflict'. A magazine
article was headed 'Woman's place is in confusion'. Their
minds may be liberated, but their emotions are still very
much bound up in their children and their partners. A
recent conference of Christian women was entitled 'Free to
be me'. When it was suggested that women can't really make
up their minds what they want, or who they want to be,
there was a terrific ground swell of assent from the
audience. Like men they do not want to be dependent, but
neither do they want so much independence that they
destroy the affection and intimacy which is the basis of their
relationship. They want to work. They also love their homes
and families, and seek what is best for them. They want to
be loved and cherished. Above all they want respect.

This can create a terrific ambivalence, and a great many
tensions and misunderstandings in the daily working out of
relationships. Men find it hard to appreciate what is going
on in their women. The women don't always know what is
going on in themselves. The vast majority reject extreme
views, and only want limited autonomy, however. 'Feminist
activity is commonly understood to aim for the inclusion of
all women in the work force and to be dedicated to the
euthanasia of monogamous marriage. Not true. The
women's movement is looking towards the wider dream of
fuller citizenship for women in a world which recognises
them as the full equals of men' (*Dispossessed Daughters of Eve*).

Equal... but different

Equality does not mean sameness either. 'Women shouldn't try to be like men, but partners,' explained one woman. 'They are equal, but different — in thoughts, looks and roles.' Another insisted, 'Women should be given consideration and treated as human beings with the same rights as men, but different emotions and physical strength.' An awful lot hinges on the vexed subject of roles. 'Women need liberty to choose where they can best function among all roles (as do men),' said a third woman. 'A lot of church teaching seems not to be Christ's teaching but a male-dominated society looking after its own best interests.'

Is this true? Is it only the fault of the men? Or have women contributed to the problem by underestimating their own abilities, and allowing men to struggle on with responsibilities and tasks they would be just as capable of fulfilling?

I sometimes feel I shall scream if I hear another lecture on the role of women. There are an endless number of roles women (and men) find themselves performing, according to their particular circumstances. Nurturing, caring, supporting, are second nature to some women. Others have qualities that make them more suited as traffic wardens, or prime ministers. To say you must conform to a certain pattern or stereotype is tampering with the uniqueness of God's creation. Of course we have to undertake certain responsibilities at certain stages, for the sake of those to whom we have promised commitment and care. In a Christ-centred household hopefully those responsibilities will not fall too heavily on one pair of shoulders.

Stereotyping

I don't see stereotypes in scripture, but an infinite variety of men and women, working, living, relating, ordering their family lives according to their ability, personalities, background, circumstances. I don't hear Jesus directing his teaching about love, service, sacrifice, the use of talents to one section of his audience only.

In her book *God and Woman* (Mowbray, 1977), Dorothy

Pape declares that 'role' is not a biblical term; that the blue-
print for God's ideal person, male or female, young or old,
married or single is that they should do his will. If dad does
the ironing, or cooks the meal, voluntarily, willingly,
because a job needs doing and he is the one with most space/
time to be able to do it, that is creating a model for the
younger generation that achieves far more than all lectures
and discussions on stereotyping. Like Christianity, attitudes
are caught, not taught, and it is not difficult to see what is
going on in some homes when you listen in the Wendy
house. 'I'm not your slave,' exploded one little girl to her
male playfellow. 'I'm not going to wait on you.'

Gradual change
Things are changing, gradually. In America the general
trend amongst the twenty to thirty age group is towards a
belief in equality, equal opportunity, and a sharing of
housework and childcare. Schools are attempting to make
pupils and publishers aware of sexist attitudes in books and
educational   materials.   Television   documentaries,
magazines and books raise issues such as how girls learn to
be women, and make gentle mockery of the various abor-
tive male attempts to prove their superiority. Even so, girls
are not really encouraged to pursue the more scientific subjects, and careers advice still tends to steer girls towards
'something to do with children', clerical work, or the service
industries. Their work is still often regarded as a stop-gap
until marriage, despite the fact that many will return after
only a few years out of the labour market, and an increasing
number may become the breadwinner for the family. Some
of the younger women seem blissfully unaware of the
battles that have been fought on their behalf, and women of
all ages continue to fight shy of responsibility, at work, in
the church, and in the home.

Strong reactions
Equal rights and individuality are threatening to any who
try to escape from freedom and choice through rigid
authoritarian direction. Both fascists and communists have

attempted to stamp out feminism, and there is strong opposition from some sections of the Church. 'Women's Lib is not your friend,' declared a well known American preacher at a conference on the family. He was teaching that women should be joyfully submissive, accepting their position in a chain of hierarchy with the husband as the head. 'Nonsense,' snapped an equally vehement female evangelist from the same continent. 'Christ is the head of the house, husband and wife are both equally responsible to him.' 'The males are dominant in most species throughout history,' blustered a beleaguered male. 'Isn't it about time they changed, then? Grew beyond such animal reactions?' challenged a female obviously used to dealing with such responses.

Example of Jesus

She could have reminded him how Jesus reversed such attitudes and values in his life and his teaching. The qualities he exhibited somehow manage to combine female and male characteristics. We see his gentleness with the children, his compassion for lepers, his protectiveness towards the weak, the poor, the underprivileged. He shared the joy of the wedding at Cana, the sorrow of Martha and Mary at their brother's death. He expressed anger when so-called leaders distorted the truth, and strength and self-discipline (which could have been construed as weakness) when faced with betrayal, trial and crucifixion. Forgiveness, wholeness, and reconciliation are the essence of his gospel. Each individual is of value. Like the lost sheep, the lost coin, the lost son (or daughter) is precious to God, and he is not happy until we are safe in his love.

If God so values each individual is it really surprising that women feel hurt and rejected when the Church, or their menfolk, try to push them back into a sub-Christian stereotype? Having once discovered the freedom that Christ gives, can they ever be content to accept a bondage which implies they are not really as valuable as Jesus led them to believe?

Male/female relationships

Should women pull back because the balance of power in male/female relationships has altered so drastically that it has outstripped the resources of couples to operate the 'massive social and psychological changes' required? Men have been trying to prove they are superior for thousands of years. They resent female independence, prefer traditional roles, and regard the changes that have taken place in the last couple of decades as a 'breach of contract'.

In that respect women's emancipation is contributing to marriage breakdown. Does that mean women should deny themselves, yet again, as expected, or can men respond to the challenge and discover their own true worth, the real authority and leadership which comes from service and self giving rather than domination? As Christ taught, 'We love because he first loved us.' If we could get that kind of thinking back into our relationships there would be less need for manipulation, wheedling, and all the other power games we force one another to play. Both the marriage service and Ephesians 5 are based on mutual commitment, the giving of one to the other. So where do we go wrong? Do we need to replace that overworked phrase 'I love you' with 'I respect you'? In other words I respect the fact that you are an individual, of equal worth, with exactly the same kinds of needs to grow, develop, express yourself as I have. It is arrogant to assume that my needs should take precedence over yours. We did not promise that, and we will destroy one another if we expect it. Somehow we have to hammer out how we two (independent I's) learn to be one (interdependent) while still retaining our individuality and identity. 'The more authentically a woman, or a man, is free to know, and become herself or himself, the more surely, uniquely she is herself, he is himself,' writes Betty Friedan in her new book about living with equality. 'The second stage is not unisex. It is human sex.'

Future potential

If we can get the base right we could release terrific potential into our homes, our churches, our community. And if

Christians cannot get it right with all the extra resources of forgiveness, reconciliation, the enabling power of the Holy Spirit, who can? It is not easy. Relationships rarely are. There will always be conflicting values and interests. Now that some of our most deeply held assumptions are being challenged it is bound to take time to adjust. Men will continue to feel threatened. Women over-react in order to prove their point. There will be a continuing need for counselling, support, understanding of what is going on. Some will retreat into known patterns. Others go under because there is no one to guide them, help them. Learning to live with equality may come more by evolution than by revolution, but it will be no less painful. Already researchers are staggered by the 'unprecedented and totally unpredicted improvement in the psychological well being of women on a massive scale' (Betty Friedan, *The Second Stage*, Michael Joseph) but concerned about younger women who show some signs of stress because of the many choices facing them.

Can men become their allies, partners, co-workers in the search to reconcile the need for freedom with the equally valid need for love, children, family, home? Are the two in opposition, or can men and women working together restructure institutions and attitudes to work, childcare and the home, and transform the nature of power? Can men find liberation from the attitudes and conditioning that bind them inside themselves? After a twenty year backlog it seems as if they are at last beginning to realize that some of the questions women have been asking may actually be valid. Will it take another two decades for them to find a new sense of worth and values? Will women begin to acknowledge their own contribution to some of the misunderstandings and tensions, and not see men always as the scapegoat for problems which go much deeper? Will the Church be able to free itself from some of the destructive views it has of women, or will it continue to deny the 'Christian doctrine of the equal worth of every human soul and of the remembered equality of women in the early Church'? (*The Subversive Family*, Ferdinand Mount, Cape, 1982).

It will be interesting to see if the American sociologist William Goode's prediction comes true. 'Males will stubbornly resist, but reluctantly adjust; because women will continue to want equality and will be unhappy if they do not get it, because men on the average will prefer that their women be happy; because neither will find an adequate substitute for the other sex; because neither will be able to find an alternative social system' (quoted Betty Friedan, *The Second Stage*).

7

Husbands and wives

So, if we can't live without them, but it's tough going learning to live with them, where do we go from there? What are the factors that make so many rush into a new marriage, or relationship, despite all the pain that may have been associated with their previous experience?

Companionship
What is the basis of a good relationship? Sex? Children? Economic stability? All these things are important but the over-riding attribute is described variously as friendship, companionship, sharing. Is this a new notion? An impossible ideal? It's been round long enough. Back to Genesis 2, 'It is not good that the man should be alone. I will make him a helpmate.' (Jerusalem Bible).

Partnership
With sublime lack of awareness of the present situation, and the Church's own specific contribution to fouling things up, Vatican II describes it as 'an intimate partnership of life and love'. As its title might suggest, *The Human Paradox* by Anthony Mann (NMGC) takes a more realistic line. 'Marriage at its best is a creative partnership of two people who are free to give and receive, at its worst a living hell of imprisonment and torture.'

We have only to look at the Bible to realize the truth of that statement. What kind of relationship must have existed between Isaac and Rebecca if she could encourage her son to deceive his father? How many insults did Sarah and Abraham exchange when year after year the promised baby failed to put in an appearance? What kind of agonies did Peter's wife face when her husband abandoned his work

and family to follow an itinerant preacher whose provoca-
tive statements could only have one end? We catch only
glimpses of the conflicts behind the scenes but they are
sufficient to reassure us that the great heroes of Christianity
were no less fallible than you or I.

Two into one

We hear a lot nowadays about incompatibility. There are
quizzes designed to test how suited you are to your partner,
danger spots to ignore at your peril. By virtue of the very
fact that marriage involves two I's it is debatable how far any
couples can be compatible. Of course there are extreme
examples. The ones where it is obvious to everyone but the
couple involved that they will never make a go of it, their
values and attitudes are such poles apart. The rest of us
have only that central core of I to contend with — I want, I
won't, I don't, why should I. How do we move from that
kind of thinking into a true partnership?

'Partnership is a voluntary unit formed between two or
more people acting from a common base of respect and
trust, recognizing each other's rights and conscious of each
other's differences, sacrificing equally and working together within a pattern they set for themselves, towards a
common goal, each contributing to the best of her or his
abilities to achieve what no one of them could have achieved
alone,' concluded the partnership groups of the World
Council of Churches consultation on sexism, 1974.

Assumptions

When those expectations are applied to marriage relationship it seems hardly surprising that only a minute percen-
tage manage to attain their objective. Marriage is not easy. It
never has been. It never will be, especially now so many of
the social, legal, and religious restraints have been removed. In a modern marriage based on quality of relationship, rather than ownership, nothing can be taken for
granted. 'When I got married the women in my office automatically assumed I would be rushing home to cook supper,' sighed one wife. 'But I never cooked for him before we

were married, and I never have since. There's always ham
or eggs or something in the fridge. It's the same if we have a
visitor. When it's time for a cup of coffee I'm the one who's
expected to go out to the kitchen, no matter how interesting
the conversation. When I raised the subject he saw the
justice of it. It was just that he had never questioned the situation. So much is assumed.'

Communication
That couple have no problem in articulating their feelings
and appreciating the other's point of view, but what
happens in the many homes where partners are not able to
express themselves adequately, or to negotiate their way
through misunderstandings? An all too common complaint
is the tragic 'He/she won't listen. I can't talk to him/her.'

Learning how to communicate must be one of the most
urgent tasks facing society. It affects parents and children,
workers and employers, governments and people, as well as
husbands and wives.

An American survey came to the conclusion that the
couples who communicate, share, and are sensitive to each
other's needs are least likely to seek a divorce. In a questionnaire aimed at discovering what kept couples together the
two main reasons they gave for being able to overcome their
difficulties were talking to one another, and talking to their
father in heaven. In other words Christians have an extra
resource to help them see beyond their own I, to the needs
of the other.

'Marriage requires consideration and compromise. It
should be a partnership in which individual selfishness is
surrendered for mutual gain. It requires a great deal of
patience, and the willingness never to give up,' says Edward
Ford in *Why Marriage?* (Argus, Illinois, 1974). 'The happiness you receive from marriage is in direct proportion to
the energies you put forth to make the thing work.'

In love, or loving
It is no use eternally hoping that a change of home, another
baby, or an increase in salary will solve the problems. The

answer has to be in ourselves and our attitudes. When marital satisfaction declines, as it does, the transfer from being 'in love' to loving is crucial.

'We bandy about the word love without realizing how much effort is required in sustaining it,' said Jack Dominian in an article in the *Sunday Express*. Couples who are working hard at their marriages described being in love as feeling, illusion, a rosy glow, romance, self-centred, physical, shallow, transitory. 'Loving puts being in love into practice,' said one of them. In what way? Their replies included giving, sharing, perseverance, hard work, accepting the partner as he/she really is, and by coping with the difficulties of living and working together.

'Being in love is a smile over a glass of wine,' said a forty-year-old mother with four children. 'Loving is a smile over the washing up.' Having watched their father dying of stomach cancer, our children now know beyond doubt that it takes more than a rosy glow or a good sexual relationship to carry you through the tough times. 'Everyone told me marriage was hard,' said a vicar's wife. 'But I had no idea how hard it would be.'

First five years
During the first five years the adjustments can be overwhelming. There are in-laws to consider, the financial strain of setting up home, a change in roles, the transition from the honeymoon period to an everyday relationship, realization of the extent of the commitment and the demands it makes. I always joked that my husband and I were only children so we hadn't even had brothers and sisters to knock off the rough edges. In reality it was no joke. 'I never knew what a nasty person I was until I got married,' grieved a friend after the first few months of marriage.

When children arrive there are extra demands on money, time, commitment. The arrival of the first baby, far from cementing a relationship, as is commonly supposed, is more likely to expose all the cracks. Young parents can be plagued by feelings of inadequacy, failure, guilt, anxiety and that terrible tiredness which leaves little time or energy for each other.

Middle years

The middle years bring a different set of problems. Often the husband and/or wife are going through some form of identity crisis. The wife may be finding a new delight in her return to work, just at a time when the husband is passing the peak of his career, or beginning to question what he has achieved in life. It is a time of insecurity, and reassessment, and often coincides with teenage crises, children leaving home, and increased responsibility, or concern about elderly parents. After several years of concern about teenage marriages being at risk, there are increasing fears for those facing the twenty-year itch.

Even when the later years are reached there is no guarantee of perfection at last. Retirement or redundancy bring a new lifestyle, and attitudes have to be adjusted yet again. As one dear eighty-year-old commented, 'Every year is different, and they all bring their own set of problems.'

Extra pressures for the Christians

The problems may be practical, emotional, psychological, sexual or financial, and Christians are not immune. The very fact that our first allegiance is to God can create all kinds of conflicting loyalties and priorities. It is far too easy to become over-involved in the Church, or work, or other people's problems and be blissfully unaware of the ones piling up on our own door step. 'If it had been another woman I would have scratched her eyes out,' one young mum said vehemently, expressing the anger she felt about her husband's commitment to the Church.

When asked how they keep a balance between the conflicting demands of partner, children, parents, church, work and the community, a terrific number of people reply 'with difficulty'. Many people would identify with the comment, 'I run as fast as I can but I never keep up.'

Balancing act

It is a constant balancing act, and whether or not the whole lot topples seems to depend on planning, organization, common sense, awareness, assessment of priorities, trial and error, and setting limits to the extent of outside involvement. A system that seems satisfactory when the children are toddlers may be disastrous when they are in their teens. How one family plan their priorities can be very different from the family in the next pew. We cannot prove our commitment to God by the number of meetings we manage to notch up each week, especially if that involves our children suffering from 'inadequate fathering', or mothering. There are too many children from Christian families carrying enormous chips on their shoulders because their parent(s) were so involved with activities and other people that they never had sufficient time for their cares and concerns. Maybe we need to re-write the parable of the sheep and goats (Matt. 25) as a parable for today's family. 'When I was upset you cuddled me. When I was tired you read me a story. When I was worried about school, or girl or boy friend problems you listened, and you understood.'

Priorities
It is no use shelving responsibility for the outcome onto the Creator when he has already given us brains and emotions to sort out the implications of our actions for ourselves. There is a tension between the demands of family and church and work; parents, grandparents and children. Trying to get, and keep, a balance is one of the major problems facing families today. There are no short cuts, or easy options. Each of us has to bring our commitments, our egos constantly before God to ask why am I doing this, what is its value compared to the enormous influence I have, or should be having, on my partner and children? Is it really necessary, or is it a cop-out from the much more costly involvement of close relationship? And, conversely, am I hiding behind the excuse of family commitments because I don't want to be too closely identified, or involved, with Christian activity?

Conflicting loyalties
Family life has been compared to a wheel with husband and wife at the centre, then the children, then the reaching out

to others. If those inner relationships are out of true everything else becomes flawed and distorted. Instead of two working together, and finding incredible strength to serve others, relationships become soured, resentments simmer beneath the surface, and sooner or later the flaws begin to show. Of course if we are Christians our first commitment is to our Master. Inevitably he calls us to serve him in our work, our community, our church. Does it have to be at the expense of the family? Unlike biblical times we no longer have the extended family living near enough to compensate for deficiencies in parenting, or partnering. How aware is your fellowship of the strains too much responsibility or involvement may be putting on the families of those in leadership positions? What action is being taken to compensate, sustain, sort out the problem? We make very serious promises to our partners in marriage, and to our children if we have brought them before God in dedication or Baptism. How often do we check that we are not ratting on our part of the bargain?

Relationship skills
Few families are not feeling the strains of modern living, but there are specific skills that can be learned about relationships, conflict, communication. Where are the courses on those skills? How many parishes come to grips with such topics in their marriage preparation and support programmes? 'Communication is a matter of conveying inner needs to each other,' says Jack Dominian. What are your partner's inner needs? Does he/she understand yours? How would you even start expressing them? Would your other half listen? Who could help you overcome the blocks to communication? Because there are so many changes taking place in society, and in the marriage relationship it is essential that we do learn to talk; to express our needs, hurts, dreams, anxieties. There are no blueprints for a successful marriage. We are all unique. We can only chart out the progress of our relationship by trial and error, give and take. It is tough, but it is unavoidable. Marriages are not static. They are made by two people, and people change.

They mature at different rates. They have to learn to adjust, for the success or failure of their relationship depends on their ability to adapt.

Change

And here comes the crunch. We all find change difficult, especially the male of the species. Even the younger ones have far more traditional notions than women. They are more 'thing oriented' than person oriented, and have great difficulty expressing what they really feel. 'If male-female relationships are to improve notably, means will have to be found to help men deal with their fears of women in more openly threat free communicate ways,' says a contributor to the book *Marriage and Alternatives*. 'Most males do not like to admit they are emotional cowards.' Of course these are sweeping generalizations and there are individual men who are able to get beyond these barriers, just as there are women who are totally unsuited to housework. The fact remains that we still have an awful lot to learn about the things that make each other tick.

Women have changed. They have 'grown up'. Like the black community they are beginning to be proud of their identity, and kick against anything that could undercut their hard won self respect. But they are fighting centuries of ingrained assumptions, in themselves and in their partners, and there are bound to be tensions and misunderstandings.

Give and take

'To achieve a successful marital partnership is probably the most difficult of life's social requirements,' according to Dr P.D. Scott in *Webs of Violence* (Routledge & Kegan Paul, 1978). To be successful each marital partner must often defer to the other... Failure to show this capacity to defer or to be unselfish inevitably leads to conflict, and conflict can easily build up to the point of violence. It is... realistic to assume that marital conflict is always a possibility in every marriage, and that it will occur when the difference in individual needs between partners exceeds their capacity to adapt.'

Conflict

The problem lies in knowing how much conflict is normal, and for many Christians, even accepting that some degree of conflict is inevitable. If the fruits of the Spirit are love, joy, peace, where does that leave you when you've just had to bawl out the kids, turned away an over-demanding neighbour, tripped over the dog, and sworn at your husband? Maybe it helps to remember that conflict is only a difference of opinion. That sounds much less intimidating, and very much part and parcel of human relationships as Paul and Peter discovered in the early decades of Christianity. Think how much scope it leaves to develop those two valuable assets, forgiveness and reconciliation, too. 'Problem solving is not to be regarded as an exceptional unwelcome activity within marriage, but part of its central texture,' states a report *Marriage and the Family in Britain Today* (Church Information Office).

Two sets of variables

And problems there will be, with finance, work (or lack of it), children, in-laws, personality clashes, different expectations, emotional ups and downs, and the constant tension between our dependence on others, and our need for independence.

The time when the last set of variables clash creates particular problems in this age of emancipated women. It is so easy to be irritated by the 'little boy' in our partner, instead of remembering however mature or independent we may be there are still times when we stand just as much in need of his love and protectiveness. Now that so many values and norms have been overturned we have got to keep the lines of communication open, to ask 'What's going on in you? What's going on in me? How do we work this thing through?'

Opting out

I know from painful experience how much easier it is to theorize than to put into practice. But what are the options? Breakdown of communications? Breakdown of the marriage? Breakdown of one, or both, partners? A divided home? If we are to get this marriage business right we have got to face and work at the problems. It's the 'grass is greener' mentality that creates the heartaches, the opting out, looking for alternatives, the 'my wife/husband doesn't understand me' syndrome. It's so much easier to unburden to a sympathetic ear, than to come to grips with the hostilities that divide the original partnership. The Ken/Deirdre split on *Coronation Street* had half the country riveted to their seats. A lot of people awaited the outcome with bated breath for it reflected very accurately the disenchantment that can set in, and the terrible temptation to seek consolation elsewhere. 'There is nothing new about dissatisfaction in marriage,' said Sean Day-Lewis reviewing a BBC 2 production *Intimate Relations*, 'Only the increasing determination to escape rather than live with it.' When Ken and Deirdre fought through their problems you could almost hear the nationwide sigh of relief.

Divorce

As many have discovered only when it is too late, opting out often means merely exchanging one set of problems for another. Life as a single parent is far from easy. Remarriage involves a lot of heart searching, and negotiation for children and adults. In an article in *Woman's Realm* Dr Jack Dominian said, 'There is at last a growing awareness that divorce, however civilized it may seem, isn't the easy solution it was once supposed to be and that there are problems about children and second marriages.'

One of the major tasks facing those concerned about the state of marriage and the number of break-ups, is to make people aware of the destructive effects of divorce, and to help them plough into their marriages the kind of effort, energy and interest they would have to employ to establish a new relationship.

Prevention

But this would involve a great many resources. Befriending, counselling, courses, seminars, books, involvement, lis-

tening. However inadequate people may feel their contribution is, never underestimate the value of a listening
ear. It doesn't necessarily matter if you haven't any answers.
In fact glib responses or advice can be positively counter-
productive. Often all people need is the feeling that someone understands, and just expressing their thoughts out
loud may help to clear their mind.

The saddest cases are the ones who know they need help
but have no one to turn to. The editor of a Christian
magazine said a lot of people write to them with personal
problems because they have no one locally able or willing to
help. In our area there is a two month waiting list to see a
marriage guidance counsellor. And that is just the tip of the
iceberg. Only a tiny proportion ever get as far as their
doors. A lot more could be done in terms of marriage
preparation, but an even more urgent need is marriage
support. It is not sufficient to have family worship and
mother and toddler clubs. We need to get to grips with the
issues which are dividing families, be aware of the pressures
on couples and individuals. If our fellowship is to be anything worth it will be on the level of listening, befriending,
sharing in the perplexities, seeking a way through, together.

Expectations

Despite the ever increasing divorce figures most couples
hope for a good relationship. They enter marriage with the
expectation that it will be for life. When I asked people if
they would still get married if they had their time over again
84 per cent answered 'Yes' and 86 per cent would still have
children. Similarly the vast majority of young adults would
like to get married, and have children. There is still a
strong, instinctive belief that two are stronger than one,
despite all the complications. 'What are they beefing about?'
a number of single people and heads of one-parent families
exploded after a discussion panel on marriage relationships. 'At least they've got someone.'

Do we expect too much of our partners, or get too discouraged by the minor skirmishes which are a normal part

of family life? All the couples I would describe as happily married have their fair share of problems, conflicts, misunderstandings.

Love/hate relationship

A modern novel about the love/hate relationship that is more commonly known as marriage has the apt title *Rough Strife*. Is such a concept too alien for the Christian community to grasp or does it actually portray the complexity and mystery of the marriage relationship? As the apostle Paul pointed out, the husband/wife relationship is in many ways a reflection of our relationship with God. We don't always dwell on the mountain top with him. Why should we expect more then of marriage? Sometimes it is good, sometimes very shaky. It can be chaotic, boring, amusing, painful. If it was dependent on our feelings it would be disastrous, and hardly likely to last more than a week.

Where there is commitment, covenant, that is the bedrock from which strength and security can grow. A Catholic priest used the illustration of Hosea as an image of God's love, and the kind of response he expect from his followers. The story is not of fresh idyllic first love, but about a battle-scarred couple coping with many failures. Can we have a few more sermons and discussions on that kind of theme, please? And a greater willingness amongst couples to admit that's what marriage is all about.

8

Parents and children

'I don't think we should have any children,' explained an attractive woman in her mid-twenties. 'I don't think I'd be able to cope.' She is probably right, but there is still likely to be enormous pressure on her from grandparents, and a society geared to asking 'Isn't it time we heard the patter of tiny feet?' an appropriate number of months after the wedding day.

Such a choice would be regarded as a 'mature, responsible decision' by many concerned about child welfare, but it is certainly not a soft option. Older women who never had to consider such a choice express relief that they were not faced with the searching self-assessment that kind of decision entails.

In Christian circles children have been regarded as a gift of the Lord, and one of the reasons given for marriage is the procreation of children. Contraception is still disapproved by some sections of the Church hierarchy. However fine the theories the laity, faced with the practicalities of day to day living, seem to have reached their own conclusion, that to produce unwanted human beings is selfish and irresponsible. Apart from concern about over-population, and financial restraints, the long term consequences of unwanted pregnancies can be resentment and violence.

Choice to have children
The choice to have children is regarded as the biggest and most far-reaching decision a couple can make. The length of the commitment is so daunting for a start. It has been pointed out that we can have ex-spouses and ex-jobs, but not ex-children. Becoming a parent is a major turning point for most people. Once the initial joy that a child has come

into the world begins to abate realization of the responsibility starts to sink in. Loss of freedom and privacy, and the cost and demands of a young child can come as a nasty shock to couples used to 'doing their own thing'. 'It seems that many people do not remotely anticipate the impact of parenthood on their lives,' say the Rapoports in *Fathers, Mothers and Others* (Routledge & Kegan Paul, 1977). It's true too. When a colleague rang to announce the birth of their first baby he said he was 'shattered' by being up all night. It was with some difficulty that I restrained myself from saying 'Don't worry. Your problems are only just beginning.' Another friend flopped exhausted into the armchair when his baby was a couple of weeks old. 'Is it always like this?' he sighed despairingly.

It has been suggested that the father's presence at the birth of his child is one of the most powerful arguments in favour of birth control. Maybe as fathers become more involved in the sheer hard work of caring for young infants it will have a similar effect.

Having, and caring for, young children does involve a powerful transition to maturity and it has been suggested that only those with a strong motivation should undertake it.

The first baby
At the moment ante-natal care may prepare the mother physically for the birth of the child, but the emotional, social and psychological aspects of parenting are woefully neglected. Numerous baby books give detailed instructions about layettes, exercises, breast v. bottle feeding, and childhood ailments but little or no explanation about what to do when a baby has howled for what seems like hours, nothing will pacify it, and something inside you is about to snap.

I have mixed feelings about the modern trend towards a short stay in hospital after delivery. Giving birth to a baby is no joke, as the word labour implies. Even the toughest can suffer from 'baby blues' or post-natal depression, and young, and not so young, mums need a little 'mothering' themselves, rather than immediate return to all the administration and organization required to run a household, to say nothing of the newcomer.

Shock to the system

Feelings are often ambivalent; intense wonder and pride, aligned with inadequacy, fear and a great deal of frustration. How do you cook supper for your husband, and bath the baby at the same time? Why does she always have to fill her nappy, or be sick, just as you are about to rush out to clinic? How do you know if the screams mean she is under-fed or over-fed?

Somehow the baby books never seem to concern themselves with such trivia. In them babies conform to a four-hour clock, leaving you ample time to clean the house, wash your hair, and have an afternoon nap. Ha! I swallowed the propaganda so wholeheartedly I was quite convinced I would be able to do a postal degree when I was at home all day with 'nothing to do'. It took seven years, several bottles of tranquillizers, and a sense of humour to come to some kind of reluctant acceptance of the reality.

Apparently I am not alone. A study between the years 1951-56 came to the conclusion that mothers with profess-ional training and experience suffered 'extensive' and 'severe' crises in every case. Young, educated mothers have even been described as a 'social problem', and their dissatis-faction is felt to rebound on their husband and their child-ren. It seems that the problem may not be confined to this group alone, however. Other research has discovered that half the mothers of pre-school children were suffering from depression. Parenthood involves such a radical change in lifestyle, finance and relationships. The woman has probably given up her job, misses her workmates and finds the new life marked by isolation, routine and frustra-tion. The wife needs the 'attentive presence of the husband when she gives up work for babies,' says Jack Dominian in *Marriage, Faith and Love*. Otherwise she gets a 'sense of being uncared for and unloved'.

The husband may also find he has problems if his wife has little time or energy for him after coping with the 'screaming thing' which seems to have taken over her whole life. The burden of financial responsibility can also weigh heavily with unemployment or a reduction in working hours affecting an increasing number of households.

Maternal instinct

A lot of damage has been done by the romanticizing of parenthood, especially the sacred ideal of motherhood centred on Mary, the mother of Jesus. It would be interesting to know how these illusions first gained credibility for I can see little scripture to indicate that Mary felt anything other than the usual ambivalence towards her firstborn. The sorrow which Simeon prophesied would pierce her heart like a sharp sword, could never have been far from the surface as she thought deeply about the circumstances surrounding his birth, and the effect his ministry was having on the people and the religious leaders.

Maternal instinct is a concept which has been greatly overworked. However much people like children there is no guarantee that some switch will flick automatically at childbirth. Neither is motherly feeling sufficient to carry you through the disturbed nights and disorder which are only part of this totally demanding job. 'It's always assumed that because you're a mother you will be motherly,' sighed a curate's wife. 'The males have got no patience and very little interest. What makes them think women feel any differently?' 'There are many women who ought never to have children, who don't want them, and who only have them because motherhood is expected of them,' says Jean Renvoize in *Webs of Violence* (Routledge & Kegan Paul, 1978) 'If television adverts showing bubbling little cherubs and helpful little toddlers were to be replaced by film of piles of dirty nappies and jealous toddlers squabbling endlessly — then perhaps young women might be less tempted to rush into motherhood.'

Mother's love

Whether they rush, reluctantly accept, or make a responsible decision, the reality of life with a new baby is often very different from their fond imaginings. It is then that a mother's love, or the love of a parent, has to be learnt. This is not a matter of feeling, but of will. Because it wants the good of the other there is strength to cope with the 'unreasonable care' demanded by a young child. Babies need food, shelter, warmth, affection and security, and it is this last requirement which generates so much tension. Child experts talk of bonding or attachment, the need to maintain contact with a permanent adult figure usually the mother. This is seen as the basis for all relationships the child will make later and they warn of the distress and disruption which can occur if this relationship is damaged.

The vast majority of the population seem to agree with this verdict. There is a strong feeling amongst both the older and younger generations that young children need their mother around.

A shared task?
The problems seem to have come with the assumption that such bonding involves the constant, total presence of that one person alone, which is not only daunting, but positively destructive. Before society was urbanized into small units there was always a granny or aunt or older sister to share in the task of helping the new baby feel it was valued unconditionally. When Rebecca was at her wit's end with her twin boys presumably one of the other women in Isaac's extensive household would have taken one of them off her hands for a while. Similarly it is hard to imagine Naomi staying far from her grandson after all the sadness of the intervening years. When granny lives the other side of the town, or country, it is a different story.

Father's contribution
Dad too may experience difficulty coming to terms with the fact that he is no longer the centre of attention, but rather is expected to centre his attention on the tiny newcomer with such an enormous appetite and lungs. It is not only the females who can find their identity swamped by the demands and responsibility of parenthood. Organizations

such as Family Network are now focusing on the need for
fathering groups. A typical response to parenthood is still
for the wife to be saddled with the baby while the husband
goes off drinking. Too many fathers are 'naive'. They have
little or no understanding about the radical change a baby
can make, and of the baby's needs. They may enjoy the
pleasures, and experience pride at fathering a child, but
fight shy of the responsibility. According to a Gallup Survey
one in six fathers have never looked after their child alone,
one in four never put them to bed, and one in three never
read them a story. Recent research led to the conclusion
that fathers participate in childcare more than a generation
ago, but only in the fun bits. About 5 per cent share in half
the work, but over half do nothing. Work is the general excuse, which must mean that there is still an underlying
belief that women do nothing while their partners are
slaving away in the factory or office.

   Similarly the father is still seen as the provider and disciplinarian, despite the fact that an increasing number of
women are the breadwinner for their family, and it has
been shown that women are actually the principal disciplin-
ing character.

Changing attitudes

As with male/female relationships it seems that as social conditions have changed so expectations of parenthood are
changing. Fifty years ago John Bowlby, one of the major influences on thinking about childcare, could see little need to
write about the father-child relationship, because his value
as the 'economic and emotional support' of the mother
would be taken for granted. Dr Spock, author of the parent's Bible *Baby and Childcare*, published first in 1946, saw
the father's role also as a back-up system. By 1979 he was
seeking to eliminate the 'sexist bias' and teaching that the
father's responsibility was as great as the mother's. Nowadays there is more emphasis on fathers expressing feeling
and affection although a number of writers and sociologists
still assume that fathers are not able or willing to be involved
in the lives of their children. One of the crunch issues of the

next few years could be how far men should be expected to take part in childcare and rearing. Is it yet another crack-brained idea from the Women's Lib stable, or a sound principle which has been neglected at our cost in past decades?

In pre-industrial societies men and women would often have worked alongside one another, with the children being far more involved in learning the crafts, skills and values of their elders as they participated in the everyday tasks which were essential for survival. The scriptures also see parenthood as a joint responsibility. Both the Old and New Testament remind parents of their accountability to God for the spiritual, moral, physical and intellectual development of their offspring.

Too little time

James Dobson, who has written many books on family matters, believes that lack of time is one of the greatest threats to family life, especially for Christians. Apparently mothers spend three times as much time with their children as fathers, and at the peak time for father participation, around the age of seven years, a quarter of fathers are hardly involved. Fathers may think they spend sufficient time with their children, but the actual amount can be measured in minutes, whereas the time watching television extends into hours. Is the television set a greater influence in our homes than father or mother? Where are our children obtaining their models of behaviour and relationship? If values are caught rather than taught what message are our children receiving from us? Which do we value most, money and success, or people, and that includes our own children? Are we so taken up with loving our neighbour that we ignore those upon whom we should have most influence?

Paternal deprivation

If we do, the dangers are obvious. Paternal deprivation is harmful. A lack of love, training and discipline can be crucial for boys. Juvenile delinquency is frequently related to father absence, a protest against female domination, inadequate supervision, and lack of a male model and family togetherness. There are terrific bonuses to be gained from spending time with children. When there is a proper inter-action they begin to emerge as individuals; people with their own personalities and interests. As Jesus acknow-ledged, children have a great deal to teach adults, and it is not difficult to imagine what he would feel about a 'Culture that values material objects, consumer goods, social status and its symbols' and encourage the 'pattern of father being taken out of close family involvement in this phase of active parenting' (*Fathers, Mothers and Others*, Rapoport and Rapoport, Routledge & Kegan Paul, 1977). It is so short-sighted for a start. What happens if the woman has had full responsibility and there is illness or death or divorce? How can the father take over if there is no relationship between him and his children? It is not sufficient to argue that men do not have the capacity for childrearing. Some find them-selves with no choice.

'Parenting is an option available… to men and women', conclude Rapoport and Rapoport after extensive research. 'One that both can enjoy and that in any given family might be developed in the way that suits the temperaments of the individuals concerned, rather than being divided into specialized traditional moulds. The real constraints are not biological… nor organizational… but ideas and concepts, textbooks and laws, images and expectations… all of which are alterable.'

Territorial disputes
Certainly amongst the younger generation there is an ex-pectation that if men helped to create the child, they should also share in its care. As one liberated female told her part-ner when he was beefing about the unexpected demands, 'It was your idea we should have a baby. You get on with it.' For the average male this must appear 'very strange territ-ory indeed', especially if it involves nappies, night feeds, tantrums and messed up clothes. It might help to 'change the quality of our grandchildren's lives,' but it's going to take some fairly radical rethinks on the way. Women are not

going to find the adjustments very easy either. However
much they may moan about lack of male involvement they
are likely to feel just as threatened as their partners have
been by women's lib, if the men begin to move into their territory.

Already in Sweden optional paternity leave can either be
shared between husband and wife, or be used for the father
to stay at home full-time while the wife works. Other experiments involve working part-time, or rotating the parenting
role.

Not everyone may be able, or willing to share parenting to
this extent, but the sooner it is seen as a joint responsibility
the better. Parenthood is tough and nobody (including
single-parent families) should be expected to shoulder the
burden alone.

Trials and traumas
Apart from all the practical problems it is too draining
emotionally, especially when the inevitable hassles erupt.
Rapoport and Rapoport state that every family lives with a
degree of imbalance/unresolved conflict and that 'arriving
at compromises, exchanges and settlements for families to
achieve a tolerable degree of harmony is a major part of
(the) work of parenting' (*Fathers, Mothers and Others*). If we
could learn to live with that maybe we would get less wound
up when the toddler throws a tantrum in the supermarket,
our teenagers challenge our authority at every opportunity,
and the in-betweens are asking for a clip on the backside.

We have suffered too much in the past from the ideal of
the Christian family where nobody ever loses their temper,
nobody sulks, nobody puts their elbows on the table, and
nobody answers back. There is no such thing. If there is I've
never met it, and I don't want to. I would be too disil-
lusioned. I can never thank God enough that the families I
know are just as fallible and unregenerate as my own.

Family life is about relationships. Sometimes we get it
right. Sometimes disastrously wrong. 'When we're all doing
the furry dance I think isn't this lovely. Why can't it always
be like this,' said a mother with three lively children. The

truth of the matter is encapsulated in a little badge/poster, which says 'Nobody's Perfect'. When I preached on that theme at a family service it struck an obvious chord. We all yearn for the mountain tops and forget that life usually consists more of the grey trudge over the plains. There may be a few outstanding athletes amongst us, but the rest of us stumble along as best as we can with the trainer frequently having to pick us up, dust us off, and start us all over again. It is comforting to think that when that elusive light brightens over our horizons and we crawl into his presence gasping 'I never thought I'd make it,' we shall receive not condemnation, but a welcoming hug and the gentle reminder 'I know, my child. I was there beside you.' Even the great apostle Paul could only strive after perfection and get as frustrated as the rest of us when his good intentions were defeated. We use too many glib words in our writing and preaching, have too many facile answers. If we are to get down to the nitty-gritty as Jesus did we need to give more specific challenges and guidelines, like the superb *Handbook of Today's Catholic Family* (Ligouri Publications). This spells out in everyday terms the difference between sharing and selfishness, caring versus indifference, forgiveness and hostility, and helps people to see the good in themselves, as well as the areas that need to be worked on.

Being part of a family is very much a learning process, which is why adults probably find it such tough going.

Time out
In past decades the needs of children have been the main concern, often to the detriment of the marriage relationship. Marital satisfaction is at its lowest ebb during the years of childrearing. In more recent years there has been a reluctant acknowledgement that parents are people too. Women are no longer content to live entirely through their children. They want time and space to be themselves, to reclaim their sense of identity which gets all too easily submerged by the claims of a family. How often do you hear a male complaining that he hasn't had the time to read the paper, or of teenagers so hard pressed they haven't got the time to listen

to the charts? Creative self-concern should not be beyond
the reach or expectations of anyone, particularly the one
mainly responsible for the emotional well being of the rest
of the family. 'If mum's happy we're all happy', said a teenager with remarkable perception. 'Success of parenting depends on the quality of the personality and the more complete the wholeness of the parents, the more (their children)
will benefit,' says Jack Dominian in *Marriage, Faith and Love*.
A martyred mother can make everyone's life a misery. In
the same way parents need time for each other, an evening
out, or a weekend away, sometimes without the children. Or
even the telly or the lounge to themselves for the occasional
evening.

The problems come with putting such fine theories into
practice. Everyone may agree that mum needs 'time out' but
who looks after the baby, or meets the five-year-old from
school, especially in a single-parent family? For most
women the welfare of children is still paramount, and it is
almost inevitable that mum is going to be the loser when her
needs and those of the children clash. 'Children do require
considerable basic care and attention by any acceptable
definition of children's needs,' report Rapoport and
Rapoport in *Father, Mothers and Others* (Routledge & Kegan
Paul, 1977). The demands of young children can be particularly overwhelming, and their parents must be greatly at
risk if they are left to struggle on unaided.

Unrealistic expectations
Parenthood is a peculiar kind of balancing act. There are
the physical and emotional needs of the children to consider, the responses and expectations of the parents, and
the requirements and demands of society, and the Christian
community. As a result we often end up with impossible expectations for our spouse, our children and ourselves. We
forget that Paul had problems with relationships, Jesus was
not beyond expressing justifiable wrath, and that Peter's
betrayal of his master led him to a deeper experience of
acceptance, forgiveness, and strength. Family life is basi-
cally about emotions, anger, jealousy, fear, love, hate, as

Jane Davies identifies in the excellent book *The Price of Loving* (Mowbray, 1981). The problem is so often we try to brush the unpleasant ones under the carpet.

Guilt and inadequacy

Inadequacy is a word often used by parents, whether they are worried about the baby teething, or a teenager who appears to be going off the rails. Very few ever feel they have made a good job of parenting. Our children seem to grow up and develop in spite of us, rather than because of us. We can only work within our own limits, and the extra strength God can give when we hand those limits over to him. It is a great relief that Christianity has the emphasis so much on confession and forgiveness. Every day really can be a new beginning for the Christian family.

We may find it hard to believe but few parents need to wallow in the pit of guilt and self reproach. If we have difficulty accepting ourselves, talking to other parents can help to get our problems into perspective. It's certainly saved my sanity many a day. It is a terrific reassurance to know that you are not the only one who finds it easier to handle a class of thirty than your own four, or who has given in and bought a portable television to ease some of the fights over who watches which channel.

Need for balance

According to the Rapoports, reconciling needs is of vital importance, and the search for balance is crucial. Parents and children both have needs, and families 'often need assistance in establishing and sustaining the right balance' (Rapoport and Rapoport, *Fathers, Mothers and Others*). The transition point with the arrival of the first baby, and when the mother returns to work create particular tensions. The wife may resent the limitations placed upon her by parenthood. The husband can feel threatened when mum regains some independence. 'He found it hard to cope when I went back to work, and started to have some life of my own,' explained one wife. 'But he gradually got used to it.' Now she is fighting a familiar battle with her own feelings as she

copes with an unplanned pregnancy. 'He said there'll be
four of us looking after this one,' she said. 'He and the girls
will help. It won't be like when they were small, just me
coping alone.'

Need for realism
One thing is certain. Her two girls will not be growing up
with romantic illusions about babies. By the time they reach
childcare classes at secondary school they are likely to know
more than the teacher. 'I'm never going to get married and
have children,' one twelve-year-old muttered grimly, after a
particularly trying tea-time with her younger sister. 'It's too
much like hard work.' If we could get that message across
loud and clear maybe there would be fewer marriage break-
downs, and battered or neglected babies.

Not everyone will have a younger sister to practise on, but
there are tentative moves in the direction of teaching
'parenting skills' and 'relationship skills' as part of the
school syllabus. It will mean massive re-thinks, and re-train-
ing of teachers, but in an age where it seems an increasing
number will be forced to spend a much longer proportion
of their time in the home such 'life skills' could be far more
relevant than reciting Shakespeare or studying the Romans
for the tenth time.

At the moment a lot of problems seem to exist unnecessarily. A sensible mum doing a good job of bringing up her
two young boys was still getting 'uptight' about her three-
year-old. 'He wants his own way so much and when he can't
get it he screams,' she said. 'Is that normal?' She shouldn't
have needed to ask that question.

Need of support
Where are the books, films, pamphlets, parenting groups
discussing such elementary facets of child psychology? We
need a lot more input like the ITV series, 'Understanding
Toddlers', to help parents appreciate what is going on in
their children and in themselves. Grandparents and older
friends could help, if only they did not have such short
memories. I doubt if children thirty years ago were really

the paragons of perfection the older generation fondly remember. There must have been times when they got just as irate because the baby splashed the bath water over the walls, the floor and the downstairs ceiling, or their teenage daughter spent more time studying the sixth form boys then swotting for her exams.

Whatever support is given needs to be realistic and honest, otherwise it could do more harm than good. There also needs to be more awareness that the pressures on family life in Southall are not going to be the same as those in Surbiton. Professionals particularly need to have their feet planted a little more firmly in reality. To tell a young mother panicking in case her first baby is developing eczema that he could develop into a 'poet or a musician, because it's usually the sensitive souls who develop such conditions' shows a fair lack of sensitivity on the professional's part. There also needs to be a greater realization that the care and education of children can be a shared task. At the moment professionals can make parents feel they are idiots, and parents already aware of their own inadequacies accept that assessment far too readily. There may be times when parents need professional skills and expertise. There are also instances when the professionals could profit by actually listening to the parent. Co-operation must surely be preferable to alienation.

Seeking help
Whether parents turn to their partners, their own parents, professional agencies, or anyone who will give an ear to their problems seems immaterial. What does seem important is to acknowledge that parents need help.

'Go into parenthood assuming that you can't do it alone, and you'll find yourself much better prepared for the demands of the task,' is the advice given in a book about parenting, *Ourselves and our Children*, compiled by the Boston Women's Health book collective. Few people would deny that children need affirmation, encouragement, and acceptance. In a generation where increasing numbers of couples are petrified at the thought of parenthood, or sink-

ing rapidly under the strain, parents need similar support.
'Our needing help comes from the simple fact that being
parents is hard work and nobody is born knowing how to do
it,' the Boston women continue. 'We want information, encouragement and companionship…. Seeking help when we
need it is not a sign of inadequacy but a mature first step
towards finding a solution to what is troubling us.' Formal
help can come through the health visitor or school. Sources
of voluntary assistance may be found in the library, clinic,
church, community centre or local papers. In most areas
there will be some form of pram club, playgroup, after
school club, toy library or holiday playscheme.

Self help
If not, and there is sufficient need, why not start asking a
few questions, pushing a few doors. There has been rapid
growth in the number and variety of self-help movements
over the last few years. Local social services, or Citizens
Advice Bureaux should have details of groups meeting
specific needs, such as single parents, autistic children,
hyperactive children, etc. Baby-sitting circles are only one
move away from shared childcare networks. Self help
begins with the realization that your problems are not
unique. There may be dozens of other parents in the same
predicament, in the clinic, school, supermarket, street. You
have only to listen to them talking to hear the frustrations
and anxieties coming out.

Befriending
Often all they need is someone to share those anxieties, to
befriend them. Organizations can provide buildings, lay on
lectures, organize courses. The real spadework is often
done in the one to one contacts when people can identify
their individual problems, articulate their needs. They
probably don't need advice, just the realization that somebody cares, has gone through similar kinds of things, and
emerged sane at the other end. A word of warning, however. Those whose children never put a foot astray, or who
have never experienced the feeling 'I hate kids… or men',

would be better challenging their energy in other directions.

Input
If families are to survive the pressures of the last two decades of the twentieth century a terrific amount of work is going to have to be done on assumptions and expectations, upgrading parenthood, making use of available resources, and making new resources available. Isolated mothers and single parents need to be integrated back into society, governments will have to sort out the effect of their policies. When families are comparatively worse off than they were forty years ago, and spending cuts slash through hospitals, education and social services, it is hard to believe any politician who claims he is concerned for the family.

Encouragement
Contrary to public pronouncements it is still families who are most concerned about their members. Apart from the rare exceptions parents do care about their children. They want nice clothes and toys for them. They want to give them a decent meal. They want them to do well in school, and become responsible citizens, with a decent job. It doesn't matter whether they inhabit a palace, or live under the shadow of the glueworks, their children are important to them. As parents they may make mistakes. They may swallow the lies of a materialistic society, and believe that possessions can replace people, the telly substitute for time, but on the whole they are not irresponsible. The vast majority are doing a good job, very often in impossible circumstances. They need their confidence building, gently pointing in the direction of help. 'Nobody's asking people to be ideal parents,' stated Sir Keith Joseph in an interview in the *Guardian* in 1973. 'Just good enough.'

Women particularly need reassurance that what they are doing is of value. Research indicates that the root of many problems is the low status of motherhood. It is no use telling women how vital their job of mothering is, then saying, as a local headmaster did, that mature students (i.e. teachers often coming into training after rearing a family) were less likely to be appointed to teaching jobs because they had 'no experience'. If women are to accept the current pressure to get them back into the home someone somewhere is going to have to acknowledge that bringing up children and homecare is real work.

Tax incentives, pay for 'mothercare' and credits acknowledging the skills and experience gained through parenting have all been suggested as means of improving the situation. Until there is a change in attitude it will be empty talk. If children are the principal resources of a country those who mould child psychology and development should not have to beg for spending money, or kneel on the floor to change the baby's nappy in the brand new toilets in the motorway service area.

The value of children

Despite all the difficulties, all the problems, anyone who has had close contact with children knows the invaluable lessons they can teach. Their energy and questions may be exhausting at times but it is a terrific privilege to 'rediscover the world through the eyes of a child'. Emotionally they are far less inhibited than adults, whether they are angry, frustrated, sad, worried, happy, you know it. The words 'I hate you' may pierce a sword through your inside but two minutes later they can be sitting on your lap absorbed in a story, and there is nothing quite like the welcome of a child. It is sad that so often we get bogged down with the demands that we don't fully appreciate how much our children give to us, or mean to us, until it's too late. A great many parents have difficulty in adjusting to the 'empty nest' when their offspring leave home, and it is reckoned that parents never fully recover from the death of a child.

However reluctant we may be to admit it, so much of our future is bound up in our children. They are part of our immortality, a positive commitment to life. That is why we have to be so careful that we do not lay upon them our unfulfilled dreams and ambitions. They give us social identity, power and influence. They are some form of security, of economic help, however unlikely that may seem at some stages of their development.

Distortions and reflections

Seeing babies turn into people who are individual and unique can bring a great deal of heartache if their individuality is at odds with our own. It can also mean we experience sharing in a deep level of creativity. In many ways the Church has been equally ambivalent in its attitude and approach to children. There have been those who have concentrated on the innocence of childhood. Others have seen children as wilful, sinful, needing to be suppressed. Maybe we need to remember our own reactions to our Father in heaven, if we are to get beyond this false polarization, our dependency, our wilfulness, our need to be loved, our tendency to go our own way. 'Pastoral care is needed to assist parents to see that giving their children an affirmative experience of feeling lovable is acting as God does with his people,' says Jack Dominian in *Marriage, Faith and Love*.

Responsibility

Is that too tall an order? Many Christian parents are aware of the responsibility. Nearly three out of four agreed with the Pope that nothing they will do in life is more important than being a Christian father or mother. Hence the feeling of inadequacy and failure if everything does not go according to plan. However much we may try to shunt the blame onto the schools, or social services, or society in general it is hard to escape from the assertion that 'It is the parents' own standards and beliefs which provide the foundation for the child's eventual conduct' (*A Fairer Future for Children*, Mia Kellmer Pringle, Macmillan, 1980). Which is probably why we get so wound up by some manifestations of teenage rebellion. We find it hard to live with our own worst faults reflected in our children.

Marriage preparation, training for life, relationship skills are vitally important. They make at least some attempt to redress our inadequacies. But they are only remedial. Where we really learn about relationships is in the home. There people see us, warts and all, free from the facade we put on for public display.

Affirmation

When a group of young people were asked what were the good things about family life their answers were all to do with relationships. Caring, sharing (the joys and problems), being interested in one another, talking, love, doing things together, supporting each other, understanding the individual, freedom, 'where no one is afraid of anyone'. The bad things were defined as lack of communication, selfishness, one-sidedness, lack of love and understanding, conflict and infidelity — to partner, God or family (i.e. putting work before home).

Helping youngsters accept and register love, and give love to others, is one of the vital functions of parents, according to Jack Dominian. Self esteem comes from feeling lovable, and receiving affirmation and praise. It has been suggested that parents should speak positively to their children at least three times for every time they speak negatively.

Interaction

There is a strong link between emotional deprivation and delinquency. The child from even the most affluent home can find anti-social behaviour a superb way of 'getting back' at parents who appear to have cared more for their own concerns than his. 'Today when closeness is more vital than ever — many children experience complete personal isolation,' says Edward Ford in *Why Marriage?* (Argus, Illinois, 1974). 'They have parents who will share a home, and food, and clothes, but who will not share the most important thing in the world to their child… they will not share themselves.'

Colour telly, stereo, video and computer games are no real substitute for someone concerned about your day, your anxieties. The Rapoports talk about children being isolated from society, living separate social lives. They are concerned that there appears to be a 'breakdown in the process of making human beings human'. Busy families are trying to counteract this problem by setting aside specific times, if only the few minutes over the evening meal, when they make a conscious effort to be available for each other. A worker for the Children's Society suggested that 'thought-ful interaction' involves time, talk, touch, ties and tasks. The scrape of the kitchen chair and a little voice piping 'I will help you' may not be the most welcome sound in the middle of the bustle to prepare the dinner, but the bonuses emerge a decade later when a rather larger person can scramble their own lunch, or prepare a celebration three-course meal.

Mutual respect
If we realized we have just as much to learn as parents as we would hope to teach our offspring, maybe we would start to get somewhere. Children have thoughts, fears, dreams, anxieties. How aware are we of what is going on in their minds? How often do we remember our own mixed thoughts and feelings in childhood and adolescence? What attempts do we make to understand their culture, listen to their opinions? How much do we respect them? 'What ulti-mately seems to be important in bringing up children to become acceptable young persons is the preservation of a degree of mutual respect as the parents inevitably cede to their children the right to have their own interests, values, and standards even when these... differ from... the parents' (*Parenting in the eighties*, National Children's Bureau).

Discipline
In many ways this is related to the vexed subject of corporal punishment. 'Parents who stress physical punishment and obedience to adult authority as an absolute value have child-ren... who are more difficult to manage than those parents who come to evolve a more democratic style of interaction based upon mutual respect' (*Parenting in the eighties*, NCB). The honour for father and mother demanded by the fifth commandment does not mean the end of any effort on the parent's part. 'Parents never drive your children to resent-ment, but in bringing them up correct them and guide them as the Lord does,' exhorted St Paul (Ephesians 6.4).

Anyone who has experienced the discipline described in Hebrews 12 knows that there is a world of difference between the anger that comes from injured pride, and the love that punishes for the child's own good.

Anger

That does not mean there will be no moments when we lash out. When a number of Christian parents were asked if they had ever feared their temper could get out of control 56 per cent answered 'Yes'. Modern day parents are not plaster saints, but 'common clay pots'. 'I think it is normal to be angry with your children sometimes, normal to feel moments of aggression that afterwards shame you when you recollect them. It is normal for people who have lost their temper to want to hit something, and it is normal for children occasionally to make their parents lose their temper' states Jean Renvoize in *Webs of Violence*. Acknowledging such feelings, and their cause, has to be 'the first step in learning how to deal with them'.

A priest described how a deeply disturbed youngster lodging in his house obviously believed all his worst fears were being realized when there was a major family blow-up. He was plainly prepared for a trip to the divorce courts and could not credit the fact that after a few days everything was back to normal. Despite our grief for how little we teach our children about Christianity they can learn invaluable lessons about faults, failure, forgiveness and the determination to work things out from even the most flawed clay pot.

The ideal family?

There is no standard pattern, or pattern of behaviour for the ideal family. Families come in all shapes and sizes, and there are many ways of being a 'good' parent. So much depends on background, circumstances, age, temperament, ability, values. There may be joint parenting, or a female head of household. The children may spend over half the year away at boarding school, or rarely venture more than two miles from base. There may be a large extended family network, as in the Asian community, or a nuclear family with only one child. They may live in a modern bungalow at a seaside resort, or on a windswept

council estate on the fringe of one of our big cities. There is
no single method that has been proved to be the way of rearing children, and no child reaches adulthood without some
problems along the way.

Attitude
What is important is attitude, the attitude of the adults towards one another, and towards the children. In a Towns-
woman survey there was almost universal agreement (86
per cent) that what contributed to a happy childhood was
not material or physical well being but 'happily married
parents'. How we achieve that happiness is the cause of
much debate, and there are several unpleasant questions
that we shelve at our peril. Is parenthood the most creative
demanding work, or routine, boring, intellectually stultify-
ing? How can we reduce some of its more negative effects?
Do children cement a marriage, or show up the cracks? Is it
possible to combine family and career? Do men take parenthood seriously enough? Does their responsibility end when
they hand over the housekeeping, or have a vasectomy? Are
women asking too much of their males by expecting them to
be more involved in the family? Will this add to the incidence of stress-related diseases amongst men in their forties
and fifties, or help them to sort out their values before it is
too late?

The cost of commitment
A discussion paper produced jointly by the NCB, NCH and
NMGC in 1982 had the title 'A Job for Life'. It traces the
education and support needed, or available, from birth
through adulthood, to being a grandparent. Parenting
really is a continuing process. One of our friends still
worries herself sick about her unmarried sons in their mid-
twenties and thirties, and a neighbour recently remarked
when I was commenting about my children, 'You wait till
you have grandchildren. They're even worse.' Happily
there does seem to be some indication of a trend away from
idealization to an awareness of the costs of parenthood.
Almost frighteningly so. A teacher in her early thirties was

obviously beginning to realize that she had to make a decision soon if she was to have a child, but had been put off by the young children she knew. 'Is it any better if you're a teacher?' she asked hopefully. I did not want to add to her fears, but neither would I have been right to offer her, or any other prospective parent, a false picture. Winifred Holtby sums up the situation superbly. 'Babies are a nuisance,' she wrote to her friend Vera Brittain (quoted in *Testament of Friendship*, Virago, 1980). 'But so does everything seem to be that is worthwhile... husbands and books and committees and being loved and everything. We have to choose between barren ease and rich unrest... or rather one does not choose. Life somehow chooses.'

9

Teenagers

'Tell me, does it get any better,' groaned a demented mum struggling to change the baby's nappy while his three-year-old sister did her bit to 'help' with the talcum powder. 'There's a brief respite,' I replied, 'In between the toddlers and the teens. Make the most of it.' You need it too, for the physical demands made by young children are as nothing compared to the emotional pressures teenagers can exert. The transition from dependence to independence can be very painful for all involved, not least for authoritarian parents. A Roman centurion had all the resources of the army and Empire to back his commands. Modern-day parents are likely to get a very different reaction from the one he would have received if they start throwing their weight around. A perceptive teenager described the children of Christian parents as 'weak and needy'. She had a point. So many seem to have had any spark of individuality crushed out of them, until the underlying resentment simmers into an almighty explosion in the teenage years.

Teenage rebellion
Why is this? Why do Christian parents find it so hard to cope with those who need to question, challenge, refute, rebel, as teenagers do? If God can accept us 'as we are' why must his followers so often try to squash his diverse creations into identical, conforming moulds? We forget too easily how often we respond to our heavenly father's demands with a 'get lost' or 'when I feel like it'. Ever since the Garden of Eden people have been exercising their free will. Is it any wonder our teenagers have to learn from their successes and mistakes that each of us is answerable for him/herself.

For a Christian parent rebellion against religion is probably the hardest to handle. It is also the one in which we need to question our own motivation most seriously. Is our concern for our child's spiritual well-being, or fear of condemnation by the Christian community if our children reject organized religion?

'Is your daughter a Christian?' someone asked after a fairly typical adolescent v. mum verbal skirmish. 'I wouldn't think so.' I shouldn't be so presumptuous. I believe only God knows where any of us stand in relationship to him, and that those who kick hardest against his control could turn out to be our present day equivalents of Paul and Peter. We seem to have lost sight of the fact that out of their defiance and failure came the twin rocks on which the early Church was built. One had to move from a position of saying 'I know' to 'I know nothing', and the other from 'I can' to 'I can do nothing', without God. Poor teenagers. All that aggro to become independent, only to find that real strength and maturity comes when we accept the discipline of the Ultimate Authority. Poor parents. Having to learn that not only can their children do without them, but they must, for a space at least.

Independence
It is ironic that the results of a job well done can so often be feelings of hurt and rejection. Giving them the freedom to make their own decisions involves frustration and anxiety. 'They can put themselves out of the reach of our direction,' remarked Ruth Hook at a conference on the family. 'Never out of the reach of our prayer.' Which is just as well, considering the numerous influences and temptations our adolescents are likely to face. Peer group pressure, alcohol, their own sexuality, choices about career, money, appearance, identity are just a few of the battles they have to fight.

What can parents do if the opposition looks as if it is about to overpower them? Put their foot down with a firm 'Thou shalt/shalt not'? Or opt out of the hassle with a bottle of tranquillizers and the telly? 'You can only reason. Then stand back and pick up the pieces,' said a social worker with the NSPCC. 'Present alternatives. Try to make them face the consequences. And allow them to be individuals... then hopefully you reduce the need to rebound,' said an experienced parent.

Alcohol

Easier said than done? Agreed. Take the question of alcohol. Do you impose a total ban, thereby pushing it into the bracket of forbidden fruit, or point out the reasons for your concern and hope the message will eventually sink in, especially when they get little co-operation, and even less sympathy when they've been sick over the carpet, or are suffering from a hangover.

How far can we utilize such gems as this comment from an article in the *Daily Telegraph* to back up our arguments. 'A Government Minister yesterday welcomed proposals by brewers to curb under-age drinking. Restriction... was based on the belief that youngsters under 18 "should not be exposed to the risk of alcohol misuse until they are old enough to recognize its potency and use it wisely".'

Sex

And what about the other powerful force, sex, which has such appalling consequences if it gets out of control. Do our reservations and restrictions come through as puritanical fuddy-duddyness, or concern that such an incredible gift should be fouled up? The permissive society may sound lighthearted, but its effects are anything but lighthearted, as Heather Jenner points out in *Marriages are Made on Earth* (David & Charles, 1979). Struggling to come to terms with our sexuality can be difficult enough at forty. Heaven help the fourteen-year-olds. My generation had nothing more serious to consider than the colour of their lipstick, and whether they had the right bus fare, when they went out on a date. A quarter of a century later sex education experts are advising teenagers to take contraceptives with them 'just in case'. Concerned parents can talk till they're blue in the face about VD, cervical cancer, and the appalling choice between abortion, adoption or an unwanted baby, but it takes a great deal of maturity to withstand the pressures, particularly for a vulnerable teenager, desperate for affection and reassurance.

Limits

However much freedom and responsibility we would hope to allow, teenagers do need limits and guidelines. The problems come with deciding which are essential, which can be negotiated, and which are downright ridiculous. 'Care without being fussy,' advises Fred Milson in *Youth in a Changing Society* (Routledge & Kegan Paul, 1972). 'Don't patronise and don't indulge.'

You cannot dictate to an eighteen-year-old, but you can point out if they cannot accept the standards and values of the home they have got an alternative. Christian parents reared on a diet of 'Gentle Jesus meek and mild' may need to examine the concept of 'tough love'. In any family there have to be rules of mutual tolerance and respect, just as there do in society. Our children will only learn to respect us and our values if we have a reason for our beliefs, and tolerance for their points of view. Do we know what they think? And why? Do we even listen to what they have to say? Ruth Hook described her experience of facing teenagers' questions as being driven back against a wall, stripped of everything she couldn't justify, and taken right down to the bedrock of her faith. Dare we face the challenge of that kind of experience?

Rejection

Adolescents do go through a stage in which they reject their childhood concept of religion, and need space and time to work through to a mature belief. They will also reject inconsistencies and hypocrisy in adults, along with adult fashions, music, reading materials, eating habits and advice. In fact it feels at times as if the only thing they will accept is money. Anyone who thinks a baby is expensive is in for a nasty shock in a few years' time. Teenagers eat more than adults, need new clothes and shoes at an alarming rate, need pocket money, money for leisure activities, school books, holidays. The list is endless.

You need a sense of humour, several safety valves, and constant reference to what you felt like as a teenager to survive in a household of adolescents. When the going gets too tough in ours I go and weed the garden or take the dog for a walk.

Generation gap

Values do change. There are different forces shaping society. My parents were teenagers during the wind-up to the Second World War. They left school at fourteen and were straightaway expected to earn their own living.

My own adolescence coincided with the 'never had it so good' era. Education was expanding, job opportunities were wide open, rock 'n' roll was in its infancy, and television and cars becoming accessible to the working classes. My own kids, growing up in the amoral eighties, face large scale unemployment, constant media manipulation, and the possibility of staying in full-time education till their mid-twenties.

The painful transition to independence can now take nearly a decade, and given the teenage unemployment statistics we could face a generation of semi-permanent cuckoos in the adult nest, and all the strains that places on adult relationships.

Effect on parents

For the traumas of adolescence are more than likely to coincide with a period of emotional upheaval often described as mid-life crisis. The years between thirty and fifty-five can bring the death of parents, the wife's return to work, the husband passing the peak of his career, and a new search for identity. Restlessness, boredom, frustration, depression, and sexual fantasies can be the hallmark of the 'menopausal male', as well as his female counterpart, and adolescent children. Yet this 'middle generation' sandwiched between the struggle for independence of their children, and the increasing dependence of their ageing parents, are expected to cope, be strong, and have no problems and needs of their own. No wonder it is described as a period of great strain. There are so many conflicting loyalties, and feelings, particularly if the younger generation appear to be making a fairly spectacular mess of 'doing their own thing'.

'Is it my fault? Have I made the right decisions? Could I have done better?' are typical manifestations of the anxiety, guilt and inadequacy, which accompany parenting through the teenage years.

When the instigators of so many of these painful emotions eventually leave home, parents are likely to experience a strange mixture of grief and relief. Women, particularly, have difficulty adapting to an 'empty nest', even though it is now normal for most married women of this age group to be in paid employment.

Support for parents

How do parents survive this traumatic time? We may not reach the extreme of the parent who had to ask for his teenager to be taken into care because of the effect on the younger members of the family, but the pressures can still be considerable. It is obvious when any group of parents get together that their over-riding concern is teenagers.

If only they could be helped to share their emotions and experiences more freely and honestly. The relief on the face of one mother when another parent assured her that the food fads and selfishness would 'pass' was enormous. There are times when most of us need to get on the phone, or out to someone who will allow us to release the emotional tension generated by living with conflicting values and life-style. Not that there are any right ways or instant solutions, but simply for reassurance we are not the only ones occasionally to wish we had practised infanticide at birth.

Communication

It is hard work trying to keep the lines of communication open. Trying to understand their way of thinking, only giving advice when essential, talking and counselling rather than laying down the law are not easy lessons to learn, even for the most saintly. Yet teenagers and parents agree that a sense of humour and continuing communication are more likely to succeed than 'heavy parents'.

Participation

Those who grow up in settings where children and families still count are able to react to their frustrations in positive ways, through constructive protest, participation and public service, the Rapoports conclude in *Fathers, Mothers and Others*. They state 'Those who come from circumstances in which the family could not function (slum or suburb)... can only strike out against an environment they have experienced as indifferent, callous, cruel and unresponsive... What is needed is a change in our patterns of living which will once again bring people back into the lives of their children and children back into the lives of people.'

This may be accomplished by something as simple (or complicated) as washing up together, or as expensive (financially) as going out to the theatre, or for a celebration meal, or a weekend away. Only the hard of hearing may be able to stay in close proximity to their youngsters (and their music) for more than a fraction of each day, but 'family time' is just as valuable in the teenage years, if not more so. In previous generations life might have been a lot tougher physically, but at least the younger generation would have spent more time sharing in the household tasks and industry. Entertainment would have been a family or community celebration, and older children would have had to share in the care of their younger brothers and sisters. How many of our churches encourage their teenage members to channel their interest in younger children into helping with clubs, or crêche, or Sunday School? How many more regard them almost as an alien breed with a dangerous tendency actually to want to use church buildings, or criticize the establishment?

Do we see their energy and enthusiasm as a great national asset, or an annoying phase that hopefully they will grow out of as soon as possible? How aware and responsive are we to their crying need to socialize; to play their records, have a cup of coffee, meet other youngsters? The Church must possess an enormous number of buildings suitable for social activities, yet the pub is probably the only place where most young people can actually go to relax with their friends.

Public image
Unfortunately, as in so many other instances, the extremes have given teenagers a bad name, and an equally bad press. A gang of yobbos on the rampage at Brighton make front page news. A survey claiming that 67 per cent of teenagers totally reject drug taking, over half consider alcohol a waste of money, and the majority still turn to mum for advice, receives thirty lines on an inside page. The hundreds of mini football fans surging outside the tube station seem nowhere near as intimidating when you remember that two of them are your own offspring, and the rest have mums who are probably just as concerned about their welfare as you.

Shared support
Professional support is only likely to be needed if parents have given up, or there is a serious problem, but groups or networks of shared support can be invaluable, however informal. Single parents particularly need practical and emotional support when their children are going through these trying years. Like all parents they need time out, evenings off, holidays sometimes without the children, someone to understand the pressures they are under, and to lessen them if possible.

Of course we worry about our children, but how often do we worry unnecessarily or about the wrong things. We forget that winding mother (or father) up is a popular teenage pastime. They can nearly always guarantee some response to that. If it's taken too seriously they can be just as taken aback as their parents, as a friend discovered when she burst into tears after a confrontation with her teenage son. 'There, there,' he soothed, patting her on the head. 'It wasn't that serious.' It is not easy being the parent of a teenager (as Mary and Joseph discovered). It does help if we remember how equally impossible it felt actually being one.

10
Living together

'What's wrong with living together? What difference does marriage make? Why shouldn't you go to bed with someone if you're not married?' demanded a youngster whose morals are largely shaped by *Dallas, Dynasty,* and her teenage contemporaries. The debate lasted for over an hour. She is still unconvinced by the arguments. She is just twelve.

Statistics
What answers do we have to what has been called 'this vexed question'? Can we afford to play the ostrich game, and hope it will go away, when all the evidence appears to be pointing to the contrary? The move to 'live-in loving' is described as one of the most drastic changes affecting marriage. It influences all social and economic classes. Between 1960-70 one in twenty marriages were preceded by cohabitation. In the years 1977-79 the figure moved to one in three. In America live-in relationships are becoming the norm on college campuses, and in a recent survey in this country only 7 per cent of the teenagers polled could see anything wrong with living together.

In one sense this is no new thing. The numbers living together have always been 'sizeable'. Common law marriages were recognized in ancient Greece and Rome, and until the thirteenth century such relationships were common in Britain. Many people simply could not afford to marry, and the community appeared to accept private contracts between two individuals, even after the Church tried to regularize relationships.

Finance
In an age of increasing dependency on state handouts finance is one of the major factors still influencing whether

a couple marry or not. Those in further education may decide the adage 'two can live as cheaply as one' contains a fair amount of truth, providing the tax man still rates them as single. Divorcees stand to lose maintenance and property if they remarry, and widows forfeit their pensions. The actual cost of a wedding now runs into four figures for even a comparatively simple celebration.

Roles

Added to this women have more legal protection and financial independence than in previous generations. A *Sunday Mirror* survey (in 1982) concluded that the woman has increasing influence on the course of a relationship. The traditional image of the dependent, submissive wife does not appear particularly attractive to liberated young females, who no longer see themselves as dependents to be handed over to another man's possession. One of the main reasons given for rejecting marriage is that sex roles appear central to that relationship, whereas personhood is often more important in a living together relationship.

Reservations

Strongest opposition to living with a partner without the blessing of Church and state comes from the ethnic and religious communities. Living together may be common terminology amongst the younger generation. 'Living in sin' is likely to be the phrase used by those with a more conventional turn of thought.

Challenges

But the young adults of today trained to question and think things out for themselves are going to need more than a 'because I/God say(s) so' to answer their 'why nots'. The whole emphasis of modern society is geared so much to instant gratification that any teaching which runs contrary to the 'take the waiting out of wanting' mentality is going to come under pretty heavy attack. Hypocrisy too will receive short shrift. Genuine concern is easily distinguishable from the 'what will the neighbours think' variety. Are live-in relationships less moral, or more honest, than those who manage to preserve a superficial image of respectability while allowing their sexuality fairly free rein on the back seat of the car, or a twice-weekly session in the bed-sit?

Only the more enslaved would applaud those who indulge in a series of casual relationships, leaving a trail of havoc in their wake. Anyone grappling to sort out how a serious relationship should progress in an age inflamed by a sex-mad media needs a very strong grasp of the hand of God, and a great deal of sympathetic understanding. In past centuries youngsters could be married and bearing children by their mid-teens. With the unemployment rate for young people as high as it is, and many others continuing in full-time education until their twenties we are asking young people to control their sexual urges for nearly another decade.

Pair bonding
There 'may be some deep-seated need to pair bond of which we are unaware,' states an American book *Marriage and alternatives*, compiled by Libby and Whitehurst (Scott, Foresman and Co, 1977). Anyone familiar with the scriptures could direct the writer straight to the creation stories. There God looks at the diversity of his creation, and it is good. The only thing which causes him to be dissatisfied is the realization that 'It is not good that the man should be alone' (Genesis 2.18).

From the beginning human beings have needed a companion, a partner. It is suggested that the main reason behind the increasing figures for cohabitation say far more about this basic urge for companionship, and the insecurity of the age, than about moral decline. So many institutions have become too large, or out of touch with real people. The problems facing our world are so enormous. Is it any wonder that when two individuals find something precious and enabling in a relationship they are going to cling to it like a man hanging on to a lifebelt, whatever their parents, or society may say. What arguments can you use to convince them they should wait three, maybe four, years before their union can receive official approval? The most likely response will be 'Why? What difference does marriage make? There's no guarantee it will last. It hasn't worked for my parents. It isn't working for my friends.'

Parental concern
Concerned adults can point out the problems, the legal, emotional, financial insecurities. Rarely nowadays can they compel their youngsters into a shotgun wedding. So how do parents react when their son or daughter say they are moving in with their girl/boy friend?
'Try to be understanding but at the same time point out the hazards.'
'Object, but couldn't prevent it.'
'Strongly advise against it. They've seen my friends and working colleagues make disasters of their lives.'
'Tell them it was wrong, contrary to God, then treat them as if married.'
'Regret it. Suffer pain. Not subscribe to their morality but still retain the relationship and be supportive where possible.'

Judgements
But how do you define morality/God's laws to a generation reared on atheistic/humanistic principles? How do you answer such questions as 'Which is offending most against God, the couple who have bought a house, have a deep commitment to one another, and have worked out their own contract for a very good relationship, or the ones who had a spectacular wedding, for all the wrong reasons, and were separated within six months?'

And what right do we have to pontificate about sexual morals if we turn a blind eye to the stockpiling of nuclear weapons, are indifferent to the three million relegated to the devastating effects of the dole queue, and do nothing to oppose the attitudes which relegate certain sections of society to second-class citizenship by virtue of their sex, race or social status? How aware are we of the restless search for

love and some form of security which so often characterizes
the children of broken homes, and deprived backgrounds?
Where are the shepherds, pastors, lights to the world who
can gently lead a lonely and bewildered generation back
into the shelter of the fold? How can we communicate the
love of the Shepherd who says 'Thou shalt/shalt not,' not
out of vindictiveness, but for our own good?

Misuse

As in so many areas maybe the message is beginning to filter
through despite the ineffective way the Church has hand-
led the whole question of sexuality. Recent publicity about
AIDS and herpes is certainly getting through to our mainly
teenage household, as is the mess a fourteen-year-old
friend has made of her life by getting herself pregnant. The
'no harm' philosophy can assume a very different face in the
VD clinic or the waiting room of an abortion agency. 'You
should hear what Christian psychiatrists and marriage
counsellors say when they are struggling to put broken
people back together again, sometimes years later,' said a
youth worker with a wide range of counselling experience.
'So many people have sexual and emotional problems because they're not using this great gift as God intended, inside a committed relationship.'

Fear of commitment

A number of cohabitees would argue against the assumption that their relationship is not committed. There are
some who are going to have problems maintaining any
form of permanent relationship, but a high proportion do
eventually marry.

One of their main hesitations appears to be fear of the
enormity of the promises contained in the marriage service
and the apparent ease with which divorce may be obtained.
How many individuals know they have sufficient resources
to meet the challenges of ill health, financial hardship, the
strain of children (and in-laws), the possibility of infidelity,
and clashes of personality and priorities, for forty, fifty,
maybe sixty years? Are the Christian ideals of lifelong fidel-

ity realistic, or 'unrealizable' in this 'tainted generation'? If
the average length of a marriage in America is now seven
years should we be thinking in terms of two levels of marriage? Mia Kellmer Pringle (of NCB) suggested the first
would have few rights and responsibilities but if there were
children that should carry a commitment to stay together
until the children are at least fifteen. At least one Anglican
bishop has also suggested the Church should lower the
entrance requirements. Would this help? Or do we need to
improve drastically our standards of teaching, preparation,
and support for marriage, and our ability to communicate
the reality of the power beyond ourselves who alone is
capable of grappling with the 'I' in us that destroys not only
our marriage relationships?

Need of limits
'It's tough enough when the two of you are Christians,'
commented a vicar's wife. 'And look at the number of
Christian marriages that are breaking down. You can only
pray "God, you brought us together, now keep us together".' For however high our ideals we still need limits,
guidelines, even the force of social disapproval, to help us in
the battle of the flesh against spirit that is so often the reality
of everyday living. Good intentions are not sufficient to
withstand the insidious and blatant seductions of the twentieth century. 'Man's inclination towards unfaithfulness and
irresponsibility makes marriage necessary,' says Paul Ram-
sey in the Grove booklet *One Flesh*. 'Society needs clarity
about human relationships. It needs to know who is
related... who accepts responsibility for the care of the
children, who owns property, and who is committed in an
enduring manner,' states Jack Dominian in *Marriage, Faith
and Love*. 'A public commitment adds strength to the motivation to work hard to sustain the relationship.'

Social customs
But social customs concerning marriage vary according to
country and culture. Are we in the middle of a cultural up-

heaval that is dispensing with the outward ceremonial on
'the wedding' and returning to a state similar to that of Old
Testament times? If a couple consent to live together, exchanging vows, agreements, even those as mundane as who
feeds the cat and pays the electricity bill, are they
announcing as serious a commitment as when Isaac took
Rebecca into his tent?

Those who have studied the subject in some depth insist
that most live-in relationships are not simply for sexual
gratification. They include an emotional and spiritual
commitment. Cohabiting couples have been described as
'emotionally' married, and many exhibit the same problems
as married couples and need counselling. A Baptist minister has suggested that if a couple indulge in casual sex they
are guilty of what the Bible calls fornication but that once
they set up home together seriously they are saying they are
married.

Total life union
Does this simply add fuel to the argument that an official
ceremony is becoming obsolete, or have we missed out on
the real significance of marriage? 'The biblical view is that
the physical union of sexual relationship is interwoven into
the life union,' says Lewis Smedes in *Sex in the Real World*
(Lion, 1976). Christian teaching about marriage comes back
time and time again to the creation story. Theologians talk
about the 'one flesh' principle. 'This at last is bone from my
bones, and flesh of my flesh,' says man in Genesis 2
(Jerusalem Bible). 'This is to be called woman, for this was
taken from man. This is why a man leaves his father and
mother and joins himself to his wife, and they become one
body.' The union between man and woman has always
been intended as the closest 'possible permanent relationship'.

When a relationship exists at this level it cannot be broken
without damage to the partners in it. Of necessity it means
that each partner gives of him/herself and takes of the
other, emotionally, physically, spiritually. If, for any
reason, that deep bond is broken there will be a feeling that

'something is missing', some part of the self has gone astray. This is why casual sexual relationships are so damaging, and why so much concern is expressed about the insecurity at the heart of a relationship as precarious as cohabitation. The marriage service contains promises of permanency, fidelity and commitment. Most couples entering marriage intend to keep those promises. The very fact that they are announcing them in public is some measure of the seriousness of their intent.

Limited liability

However much its supporters argue to the contrary there cannot be the same level of commitment in a 'live-in' relationship. The book *Marriage and Alternatives* states 'Most cohabitants will invest time and energy in a relationship as long as the rewards (satisfaction and enjoyment) outweigh the costs (sacrifices).'. This is a far cry from the commitment which promises 'For better, for worse, for richer, for poorer, in sickness and in health'. It takes more than a good sexual relationship to carry a couple through the devastating effects of redundancy, or the birth of a handicapped child.

The fact that it is based purely on private agreement implies that a 'live-in' relationship can be dissolved just as easily when there is disagreement. A cohabitee has no real legal or social status, and the relationship has been described as 'uncertain togetherness'.

Second best

There is still a widespread belief, even amongst those who practise it, that cohabitation is second best. A judge created a nationwide controversy when he branded cohabitation as having all the advantages of marriage with none of the responsibilities. If this is so far from the truth, why do so many cohabitees accept the importance of legalizing their union when they are expecting a baby? It would be tragic if material considerations were seen as the only, or most important grounds, for marriage, but the financial and legal precariousness of 'live-in' relationships become more obvious when there is a child's future to safeguard. If a woman is not married her child will be classed as illegitimate, she will be the legal guardian of any offspring, and right to property, pensions, maintenance and goods will depend on the whims of the court. Reasons for deciding to marry when a child is conceived include 'wanting stability for the child', 'a bigger commitment', and an acknowledgement that however much it may go against the grain a woman does become more economically dependent on a male when she has to care for a young child.

When a relationship is 'terminable' there must always be fear of giving the self completely, anxiety that the other could reject you in favour of a more attractive proposition. Christianity hinges on the truth that people are of tremendous value. When they are used, disposed of, broken, wounded, it is a cause of enormous grief to the heart of the Father, who sets ideals and limits, not out of contrariness, but out of concern. Those who neglect the need for a regular period of relaxation find their bodies sooner or later rebelling. When the commands about stealing and murder are ignored the most vulnerable are afraid to walk the streets after dark, and are not even safe in their own homes. Casual or self-centred attitudes towards relationships result in broken promises and broken lives.

Need of assistance
Some people may be capable of setting their own standards, of treating others with the same concern/respect they would hope to receive. An awful lot more need some form of outside assistance. If we expect people to have a 'high ideal of Christian marriage', and to exercise sexual restraint in any other relationships, what kind of teaching, reasoning, counselling, resources, are they being given to help them live with standards which are so contrary to the spirit of the age?

The New Testament teachers didn't just bewail the immorality with which their new converts were surrounded. They launched into the offensive with very practical illustrations about living in the light, putting on God's armour, respecting our bodies, and facing up to the conflicts of flesh against Spirit. How aware are we of the pressures the younger generation particularly are facing? Besides the constant barrage from the media and their peer group, there is a very real fear of nuclear holocaust, and a high likelihood of limited or no employment. If we expect them to act as saints in a sensual and insecure society we need to make sure they have more than the usual undiluted television and the pop magazine market to help them regulate their desires.

Sexual standards
Are Christians being killjoys by expecting high standards of sexual morality? Is self discipline/God's discipline outdated? Or do we need standards, codes, limits, for our own sanity, and the survival of society?

Is there something 'morally special about sexual intercourse' as Lewis Smedes, and numerous other Christian thinkers, insist?

Even the DHSS use the criteria of whether a couple are 'living together as man and wife' as the determining factor as to which benefits people should receive. 'The reason for having intercourse within marriage is not that something illicit is made licit — but rather that marriage contains the proper conditions for doing justice to sexual intercourse,' says Jack Dominian in *Marriage, Faith and Love*.

An attractive alternative?
Whatever the pros and cons, we are not going to convince the sceptics that they are 'missing out' on something good if they cannot see the evidence to back up the arguments.

'I only know one happily married couple,' a young man said wistfully.

'Only people who've had long and happy marriages will argue for it,' remarked a woman on *Time and Talk*, BBC 2, 1982.

Broken homes, lack of interest in others' concerns, lack of respect, and escalating divorce figures are going to create hunger for a deeper commitment. Much of the anti-family propaganda has already come from the destructive effects of families functioning below the level God intended.

Seeing love, power, forgiveness, reconciliation in family relationships could do the trick. If marriage and family life are to be seen as viable, attractive alternatives there has to be a massive input of energy and effort to ensure that they really are.

11

Choosing marriage

'I don't think I could ever get married,' said a woman in her late twenties. 'It would mean giving up so much.' The reasons behind such thinking include woman's hard won struggle for independence, fear of the opposite sex, career opportunities, dedication to a cause, and, occasionally an honest assessment of your own faults and foibles. Sometimes it is simply lack of opportunity. There may be no partners available in the right age/social bracket, or few opportunities to meet and socialize. Often nowadays individuals may opt for celibacy for very similar reasons to those choosing cohabitation. They are afraid of their own fallibility, and can see the fiascos other appear to be making of their marriages. It's not so much that people disagree with marriage as an institution, more an awareness that only the privileged can live up to it.

Popularity of marriage

Ninety per cent of men and women will have been married by the age of forty, and despite a temporary slowing of the marriage rate in the seventies a computer prediction states that only 2.4 per cent of young adults are not likely to marry. A youth study quoted in the American book *Marriage and Alternatives* discovered that most young people are still essentially conventional, and that very large numbers have no plan to depart from the model of preceding generations. It concluded that marriage will not change for most people, and that the majority will maintain conventional family roles. In Britain a survey in the magazine *Options* revealed that 93 per cent of those questioned still see marriage as the nucleus of a lifetime arrangement within which a family may grow, and that the majority enter it on the basis of it lasting.

Permanence and faithfulness

What factors have contributed to such an overwhelming vote in favour of marriage? The answers include security, stability, a firm foundation for a real relationship, more attempts to overcome problems and more permanence. Despite all the publicity and pressures to the contrary there remains a strong feeling that it is wrong to be unfaithful, and that once married it should be permanent. Most European countries have always been monogamous, and experiments in alternatives to marriage affect only a small proportion of the population, and are not noted for their success, stability or strengthening and maturing powers.

On the other hand the strength of marriage comes from the fact that it is a 'basis on which the challenge of change, conflicts, crises can be met and faced' (*Marriage and the Family in Britain Today*, Church Information Office). When it is working properly there is a terrific potential for sustaining, healing, growth, continuity, and expression of sexuality. To be joined with someone who knows you at the deep, intimate level of marriage, and who accepts you unconditionally, is an incredibly liberating experience.

Commitment and covenant

In one sense the marriage certificate is an irrelevance, a legal document to satisfy society's requirements. The commitment to love, honour, comfort, and cherish is the bonding factor. The world may see marriage as a contract with mutual rights and obligations, according to the society in which it takes place. The biblical view of marriage is that of a covenant, 'an agreement between two parties based on promise' (David Atkinson, *To Have and to Hold*, Collins, 1979). From the Old Testament through to the New we have repeated illustrations of this principle, God's covenant with Israel, the new covenant sealed by Jesus, each individual covenant a disciple makes with his master. Such covenants imply commitment, faithfulness, acceptance, public knowledge, and the growth of the relationship.

When we promise 'I will' do we really mean it, or do we qualify it with an unspoken 'as long as it pleases, satisfies me'? Do people have the resources in our modern world to undertake this level of commitment?

So many of the traditional bastions surrounding marriage are decreasing in importance. Law, tradition, property, money, children and social or family approval are no longer essential.

Images of love

Modern marriage is based on companionship, friendship, love. Yet where do we get our images of love? Soap opera? Romantic fiction? *Play for today*? The film industry? Sex education? No wonder the divorce courts do such a good trade. The virtues of self discipline, consideration for others and sacrifice are not often extolled by those who shape the values of the late twentieth century.

But how else do we make the transition from being two independent individuals to an interdependent partnership? When a number of married couples were asked what they expected marriage and family life to be like, they replied, 'Without conflict, like home, happy, exciting, easier, romantic, like playing house'. To cope with what it is really like had taken time, experience, maturity, give and take, hard work, willingness to admit mistakes, a sense of humour, negotiation, honesty, faith, help, trial and error, patience and 'trying to find one good thing and building from that'.

Preparation

What preparation had the couples received to help them cope with these adjustments in their thinking? Forty per cent answered 'none', 16 per cent had found books helpful, 30 per cent had undergone the traditional pre-wedding chat with the vicar. This varied from a few minutes with the curate the night before the wedding, to pre-marital counselling with an older couple over a six-week period after the couple to be married requested it as one partner had been through a divorce.

Is this adequate? What right have we to denounce the divorce figures when so little effort appears to be going into ensuring that people understand the 'stresses, strains and responsibilities of married life', and receive some kind of after care to help them cope with the inevitable adjustments? Individual churches may not have the resources or expertise, but what is wrong with a combined effort, calling on the assistance of professional counsellors and advisers wherever possible? It may only touch on potential problems, and fall on deaf ears, but at least it would be helping to promote the idea that there are people available when the going gets tough.

'The trouble is', said one rural dean, 'the clergy are too used to doing their own thing, being their own little gods. They won't co-operate.' Shame on the clergy. If marriage is 'the single most important institution for healing human wounds in society today' (Jack Dominian, *Marriage, Faith and Love*), isn't it time they stopped hiding behind irrelevancies and started to come to grips with some of the issues destroying home and family life?

Assumptions
We can no longer assume that people will learn to love in the security of their own family. If children learn by observation a lot of the messages they are receiving are not going to help them to establish secure, stable relationships in the future. The traditional family pattern with the husband as the authority figure, and the wife as the dependent, child rearing machine is also undergoing extensive overhaul. Nowadays the needs and the interdependence of the couple will be more important. In many homes there will be no father figure, or a succession of 'uncles' or 'boyfriends'.

The expectations that men and women take into marriage are also very different. Females are three times more likely to see marriage as unfair and subordinating to women, whereas few men want to strive for greater equality.

A tough assignment
Many of the basic assumptions about permanency, fidelity, procreation are under threat. Whether a marriage endures largely depends on the quality of the relationship. But

married life has always been tough, whether it was covered with a veneer of upper crust respectability as in Jane Austen's society, or the much more earthy affair of Thomas Hardy's agricultural communities. Income, education, social standing make little difference when it comes down to the battle of the two 'I's' learning to function towards a common purpose. How realistically do we spell this out to prospective partners? How much pressure do we put on young people in our churches to get married? Should we rather be telling them 'If you haven't got guts, stamina, stickability, and the ability to see as many flaws in yourself as your partner, stay out?' Jack Dominian has suggested that it should be made more difficult to get married, that there should be a twelve months' waiting period from the time notice is given with proper instruction and help and advice afterwards. Could that work? Would it not encourage an increase in cohabitation, or pre-marital sex?

Sexuality

Where are the Christian publications dealing realistically with the whole subject of sexuality in a society riddled with distortions of this incredible gift? It is very difficult to concentrate your mind on whatsoever is good, beautiful and true when you are surrounded on the tube train by page three pictures of scantily clad females, and the usual scandals about who is going to bed with whom. 'No' is not the easiest word to employ when everyone around is shouting 'Yes. Yes. Yes'.

But to regard marriage as the simplest way out of temptation is both naive and short sighted. Easier access to divorce and the number succumbing to extra-marital temptations soon put the lie to that idea. The sooner we wake up to our vulnerability in these areas, the better. At the moment the deceiver is having a field day deluding the twentieth century sons and daughters of God.

Realism v. romanticism

If that essential relationship, ordained by God, from the beginning, for all mankind, is coming under attack, is that so surprising? The question is how long is it going to be before we muster up an effective counter attack? If 93 per cent of the people interviewed for the *Options* survey are in favour of marriage but 33 per cent of marriages are failing, where are we going wrong? If love is such an essential ingredient in relationships, why are we not interpreting it in language people can understand? Married couples described it as 'ongoing, realistic, working together with the nuts and bolts of everyday life, acceptance of the other person as a human being, feeling free to allow your inner self to be exposed, the ability to live with failure as a norm', and 'being aware that both have clay feet and therefore being tolerant'.

Please can we have more books, articles, sermons, counselling material, films, plays, teaching material that spell out such specifics? Please will the couples who are making marriage work stop being apologetic about it, and start sharing the lessons they have learned, and are still learning, with those who are desperate to find a way through their tensions?

Seeking a solution

Only a small proportion of couples needing advice seek the assistance of the professional agencies such as marriage guidance. A number of Christian couples do receive counsel from clergy or elders of the Church, but by far the highest proportion go to their friends or family when they have problems. 'I would go to a friend who was married and willing to talk about how they solved their problems', is a commonly expressed feeling.

But how many of us are prepared to make ourselves vulnerable at this level, especially in Christian circles. Dare we admit that we have problems in our marriages, and that the main problem is often ourselves? Can we help others get their problems in perspective by sharing our own experiences, however painful they may be? Would we have the wisdom to see when the problems were beyond us and assist the couple to seek more expert help? How aware are we of the marriages most 'at risk' in our parish? How are we getting alongside them to support and befriend? What provision is there in your area for counselling one year into marriage, when the cracks are beginning to show? What models of healing, forgiveness, reconciliation, do people see in our homes, our church? Do they go away from our fellowship uplifted and inspired to have another go, or with a feeling of failure and condemnation?

Shouting from the sidelines

How many books and pamphlets are there on our bookstalls dealing with the 'nuts and bolts' of everyday living? People are screaming 'Come over alongside and help us'. Are we really so lost in our own power games and cloud-cuckoo-lands that we can no longer hear?

Those who choose marriage are promising faithfulness, permanence, self giving, sharing, sacrifice, perseverance. They cannot keep those vows unaided. If we believe that level of commitment is needed for the survival of society, and individual sanity, we will need to do far more than shout from the sidelines.

12

Practical involvement

If you want to know how responsive the local church is to the needs of the community you have only to walk into the buildings used for social activities during the week. If they are spotlessly clean, immaculate and empty you have your answer.

In past generations the church was the centre of the community. Too often nowadays it is on the periphery, in attitude and inclination. Is your church reaching out, releasing Christians into the community, or has it become so introverted it can no longer see beyond the dry rot, or condemnation of the new form of worship? How aware is your fellowship of the particular needs and pressures on the families in your area? What is it doing about them?

Bridges or barricades?
The Church of England Children's Society has been warning for nearly a decade that the number of two-job families will not drop, and that new measures are needed to meet this situation. It is estimated that 100,000 five to ten-year-olds spend part of their school holidays unattended, and that 9 per cent of the under-elevens, and over 40 per cent of 11-16 year olds are alone at home for part of the working day.

We can argue until the cows come home whether it is the parents' responsibility or society's to be concerned about these children. The fact remains that this situation exists. Do we view it as a bridge into the community, an opportunity for service, or yet another barricade between 'us' and 'them'? Various groups and organizations have already responded with 'latchkey' clubs, and holiday playschemes. Has your fellowship considered any possible responses to this need? The National Children's Bureau publish a help-ful booklet on latchkey clubs, and people who have already established succesful schemes would probably be happy to share their expertise.

Special needs
Similarly how is your church responding to the special needs of single-parent families? One of the saddest comments I have heard recently came from a young widow who felt very isolated in her church because she didn't know of any other single-parent families. My immediate response was they must all be in Newham, our local borough. But I know that cannot be true. So why, with rare exceptions, are they not in the church family? There is a consistent thread through the psalms, the prophets, the teaching of Jesus and the letters to young churches about the particular responsibility God's people should have towards the more needy sections of society. Now the extended family network has been weak-ened and fragmented, some needs are even more urgent.

Single parents are often desperate for adult conversa-tion, companionship, practical help and emotional support. Their children may need educational advice, a cuddle, opportunities to do little jobs to earn some extra pocket money, a few hints about how to relate/respond to the emotional needs of their parent, models to compensate in some small way for the missing parent. They will need to be included in special activities at family times, Christmas, weekends, holidays. They need people to be aware that every day can bring a new financial or emotional headache, and that the one thing they particularly lack is someone to share that burden.

A needy world
The word which keeps cropping up with unfailing regular-ity when considering the problems of present day society is need. Jesus saw a very similar situation twenty centuries ago. Social patterns and stresses may change. Human falli-bility remains pretty constant. If we are going to identify, and respond to today's needs, we have to open our eyes and

ears, just as Jesus must have done when he sat resting by the well in Samaria. The queue at the bus stop or the supermarket check-out can be just as much an opportunity for listening, praying, or offering a small encouragement to a harassed mum, as it can for raising the blood pressure. What are the people talking about in the clinic, the post office, the pub, your street? What seem to be the special points of need? How can you/your church begin to reach through to them? How can you help counteract the forces which are destroying some of them from inside? Of course we cannot be all things to all men but maybe we could do a great deal more than we are doing at present?

Inadequate excuses

When inspiration and expertise are lacking, what about studying what others are doing, not to imitate, but to spark off ideas and get people thinking. The age of sitting back expecting our pews to be filled by a quick burst of evangelical activity is long since past. The most effective 'outreach' I have seen was taking place in buildings falling apart with dry rot, heated by one oil stove, when the group could afford a gallon of paraffin. There was little preaching, but there was a good deal of identification, acceptance, welcome, and listening to the concerns of those who were coming in from the local community.

We can hide behind lack of manpower, shortage of resources, and obsolete buildings indefinitely but God has a strange habit of using the weakest and most inadequate, as Moses and the disciples discovered, and the church in many downtown areas is re-discovering. We can hardly complain about God driving us to our knees, if we refuse to learn any other way. In our area, which vies for position at the bottom of most socio/academic league tables, we have latchkey clubs, holiday playschemes, a parents centre, play association, children's centre, a hostel for the homeless, telephone helplines, special facilities for the ethnic minorities, projects for the unemployed, and numerous other groups concerned about the special needs of women, single parents and the handicapped. At the other end of the country, on the furthest tip of Wales, where unemployment has been well above the national average for a couple of decades, the local community has raised sufficient funds to rescue two halls for community use.

The importance of the individual

These initiatives must have started with someone with a germ of an idea, discussing it with another, and another, and not taking no for an answer when doors appeared to slam shut in their face. Many of the new initiatives in family support have originated with one person identifying a need, and reaching out to others with similar needs. Parents of hyperactive children, single fathers, and the association of people caring for the elderly and the disabled are just a few of the groups which have grown from someone recognizing the value of linking up with those with similar problems. The majority of pram clubs and playgroups have probably started with two or three young mums realizing that their needs were not unique. There is some evidence of new ministries to the unemployed as concerned Christians become more aware that the situation is not going to improve radically, whatever the politicians promise. Will we also see an increase in support groups for the elderly as numbers increase and welfare provisions decrease? The warning lights are already flashing. It is time to act now.

Sources of information

How familiar are we with the knowledge and expertise accumulated by organizations such as Help the Aged and Age Concern? Can we use it to help us think through the local churches' response to the needs in our area? Most of the national organizations produce pamphlets about their work, and part of their strategy is to advise and inform, whether they are concerned with poverty, cruelty to children, the elderly, the bereaved, young people, single parents or family welfare. It may be argued that the Church is not a Citizens Advice Bureau, but maybe it would be taken more seriously if it began to regain at least part of that function. People start to sit up and take notice when Christians live what they say they believe.

If involvement in matters which are tearing society apart really is beyond the scope of the local church there are still plenty of openings for people with an hour or two to spare with existing organizations. Local libraries, newspapers, laundrettes and Citizens Advice Bureaux usually carry addresses and telephone numbers of voluntary organizations who would welcome those prepared to learn a few basic skills, such as listening. Family Network, which provides a phone-in service for those with family problems, lists the qualities needed for their workers as common sense, patience, sympathy, reliability, and confidentiality. Many other voluntary organizations would endorse those requirements.

Co-ordinating resources
Besides learning to get alongside people with the idea of encouraging and supporting them, people are at long last beginning to appreciate the value of sharing or co-ordinating resources. The Women's Action branch of the Church Pastoral Aid Society are encouraging a ministry to young mothers by mailing leaders of pram clubs and mother and toddler groups with shared information and an ideas sheet. The new Christian Link Association for Single Parents (CLASP) sends a regular newsletter to members suggesting ideas for holidays, reading, etc, and publicizing local groups and their activities.

On a much larger scale Family Forum, a pressure group set up in 1980, unites the experience of over a hundred organizations, including those as diverse as Brook Advisory Centre, Catholic Marriage Advisory Council, Mothers Union, National Childminding Association, and Child Poverty Action Group. Standing committees have been studying and reporting on education for parenthood, conciliation services, the elderly, home and work responsibilities and the family and the health service.

Co-operation between churches?
Traditionally many Christian groups have been afraid, or suspicious of involvement with non-Christians, or even

other denominations. Yet we could learn so much from one
another. The Family Life Education Ecumenical Project
stresses the 'need of churches to recognize strategic roles,
and to take a more positive stance in matters relating to
marriage and family life, recommending future action
along ecumenical lines'. Already the Anglicans have in-
itiated various projects on preparation for parenthood,
marriage and personal relationships. The Baptists sold
their entire stock of a Family Life kit produced in 1979. The
Catholics have Marriage Encounter, and the National Pastoral Congress of 1980 was concerned with a strategy of
support for marriage and family life. The FLEEP Project
hopes to encourage and extend existing work, and training
opportunities for clergy and lay people. It will also research
into such things as the deterioration of the relationship with
the arrival of the first child, and the necessity of providing a
'framework of support to all married couples especially in
the early years'. Their work is described as 'not just preven-
tative, but inventive'.

Time for action
Whether the churches are able to overcome their prejudices
and respond to the challenges remains to be seen. At least
there are signs that people are becoming more aware of the
urgency of the task, and the need for new initiatives. As
many single people point out, there seems to be a prolifera-
tion of books, sermons and seminars on marriage and family matters. Hopefully they will appreciate that desperate
situations require desperate remedies.

We need more Christians involved in large-scale projects,
planning, publications. We also need to be more aware of
the enormous influence individuals can have on a one to
one basis. Often people simply need a sounding board,
somewhere they can let off steam, particularly it they are
struggling to cope alone. Just to talk about a problem
releases a terrific amount of tension. If the person befriending can organize practical help that is an added bonus, but
frequently all that is needed is a word of encouragement,
the knowledge that someone appreciates the problem, and

cares whether you sink or try to strike out for the shore.

No simple solutions

There are no easy answers to many of the pressures dividing and destroying families today. The problems will not be solved by the Government or a minister for the family, or new educational policies. They will certainly not be alleviated by those in a privileged position taking the line 'This is your problem. Sort it out for yourself, and please God don't let it affect me.' A local fringe theatre group voluntarily restrict their income to the level of what they would receive if they were on supplementary benefit, in order to identify with those who have no choice but to live on a limited income. If we are to get the good news of Emmanuel — God with us — back into the homes of our land maybe we could learn from their example, and say 'OK, you hurt. Let me share that hurt. Then maybe together we can find a solution.'

13

Is there a future for the family?

'My daughter won't go to school. She's fourteen and bigger than me. How can I make her?' 'I've been offered this job. We need the money but I can't take it. Who'd look after the kids in the holidays?' 'How can I tell my daughter her dad's gone off with another woman? She thinks the world of him. She'll blame it all on me.' 'What can I do about my mum? My dad's just died and she's all alone. It would be disastrous if she came to live with us, but I worry myself sick about her.'

When such questions are just part and parcel of everyday conversation can it really be true that people have 'given up' on the family? Doesn't it rather indicate a desperate concern to 'get it right', sometimes against overwhelming odds? A prison officer explained how the women in his charge worry enormously about their children. If you listen to the conversations in the canteen, the clinic, even the pub, invariably they turn to children and family concerns. In a 1982 poll (conducted by Gallup for Birds Eye) family life came second only to health on a barometer of life's values. Sex, leisure, success, holidays and money were way down the list.

Support system
For all its inadequacies the family is still seen as a strength, a support system. People describe it as a safe place to make mistakes, to learn about relationships, a refuge, a healing place to recover from life's hurts, a secure base, an anchor. When it is functioning properly it gives people identity, a sense of belonging, a secure base in a changing world.

One of the questions we had to consider when we applied to adopt a coloured child was 'What if she has a white boy-

149

friend when she's a teenager, and his parents refuse to have her in their house?' We replied that she would probably have to face that type of prejudice anyway, and at least she would have the family to back her up, rather than the changing personnel and impersonality of a children's home.

Children in care and from broken homes often fantasize about belonging to a conventional family unit, and the death of a parent can have a devastating effect, whether the child is thirteen or thirty. As long as mum and/or dad are around somewhere in the background there is always a feeling that somebody cares. In times of crisis the pull of the family can become most apparent. War, ill health, trouble, failure can all send us scuttling back to our bolt holes. We may have a thicker veneer of sophistication than the four-year-old wailing 'I want my mum', but the inner feelings can be identical. A social worker with the NSPCC explained how when youngsters get into trouble the only people who really care and take the heaviest weight of the burden are their families. In Japan the family is seen as the keystone for emotional security. The Jewish family reinforces the sense of identity, of belonging to a chain linking past and future. Adopted children, and those whose past has been disrupted in some way, may be particularly keen to trace their roots.

Solidarity

However fragmented modern families have become, on the whole they do still care about what happens to the members. A social worker in London's dockland described how although the extended family rarely gets together except for weddings, or funerals, when they do there is always a sense that they ought to meet more often. Similarly, if someone gets a degree or has a similar success, everyone is delighted, and bathes in the reflected glory.

Families give a feeling of solidarity, clan, us against the world. At its most basic it can be seen in the belligerent mother, or father, storming up to school to beat up the teacher who dared accuse their child of some wrongdoing.

In his book *The Subversive Family* (Cape, 1982), Ferdinand

Mount puts forward the idea that 'the family is a subversive organization... (which) is the enduring permanent enemy of all hierarchies, churches and ideologies'.

Key unit

However it may be structured 'the family, in the sense of a man and a woman living together and rearing children, is still a key institution in society' (*Happy Families*, Study Commission on the Family discussion paper, 1980). There are few cultures or societies that do not organize themselves on some kind of marriage/family structure. The basic pattern in our biological make-up urges towards some form of bonding, and no superior alternative has yet been found for the care and rearing of children.

Although many of the functions of the family have been eroded, it remains the primary source of nurture, sharing, support and socializing. Many of the problems exhibited by delinquent youngsters can be traced back, not to inadequacies in the education system or health service, or the failure of law and order, but to something lacking in their basic support system, the home. Child guidance now centres far more on the whole family.

Lasting influence

In an amusing but thought-provoking book, *Families and How to Survive Them* (Methuen, 1983), John Cleese and Robin Skynner discuss how families can make, or break, an individual.

You do not have to look far to see how an overpowering, or possessive personality can strangle or hold their children in bondage, enforcing dependence, and restricting their development. Conversely, lack of interest and involvement, and poor patterning can leave youngsters, and adults, with a feeling of rejection and bitterness.

There is much debate about the nuclear v. extended family with sociologists bewailing the fragmentation of the family into small isolated units, but an interfering and domineering matriarch can be just as destructive as trying to function in isolation. It is not so much how family units are structured that is all important, as how individuals relate inside those units, and to the rest of the world.

Potential

Whatever the imperfections of the family few people would like to see it disappear. There is a strong feeling that it may not be ideal, but it has the possibility of fulfilment for all its members. For all our mistakes Pope John Paul II said that in years to come people would call this the century of the family. In his book *The Family and Marriage in Britain* (Penguin, 1973, 3rd edition) Ronald Fletcher states 'I do not know of any other period of British history in which the qualities and expectations of marriage and parenthood — in personal, social and legal terms — were of as high a standard (and for the whole of the population) as they now are.'

Many marriage counsellors would agree with this. They are concerned because one of the main causes of marriage break-up appears to be not that people have 'given up' on marriage, but that they expect too much from it.

Alternatives

There have been various attempts to restrict, or substitute for, the family in the present century. Attempts to abolish it in Russia led to social chaos, and a reversal of the process. Members of the kibbutzim in Israel have come to the conclusion that they can 'no longer disregard so vital a human need as the desire for family affiliation' (M. Gerson, *The Family in the Kibbutz*, Journal of Child Psychology and Psychiatry, 1974).

The family continues to flourish in China, and experiments in communal living have not produced many impressive successes. In the nineteenth century the most enduring communities appear to have been those with 'powerful religious underpinning'. In Christian circles there is a new interest in communal living, but it involves a high degree of commitment and a sharing of basic ideals. It can be a terrific strength for some members, but a strain on others, particularly family units within the wider framework. Both David Watson and Tom Lees have spelt out very honestly some of the painful lessons they had to learn when they undertook this form of lifestyle.

Although living in community can help to reduce the sense of isolation and loneliness experienced by many in our fragmented society research indicates that it is unlikely to become a popular choice. Young mums might want less isolation, but not at the expense of their privacy and autonomy. They would like to feel part of a wider community, rather than participate in communal living.

Modern experiments
Other alternatives based more on sexual freedom than on ideological grounds have been attempted over the last couple of decades. Various books and films have extolled sexually open marriage, homosexual liaisons, group marriage, and swinging (or mate sharing). Statistics show that such activities involve only a minority of the population, however, and that the vast majority disapprove of such 'risky' experiments. Opponents have described them as 'a load of ungodly, selfish, humanistic, devil inspired junk', and even the more sympathetically inclined admit such liaisons often involve secrecy, jealousy, betrayal of trust, a vast output of emotional energy, and are 'not for the naive'. 'The area of sexuality outside of marriage is still a grey area which may create anxiety, sense of loss, and complex problems for spouses', states one of the contributors to the book *Marriage and Alternatives*.

Serial marriage
On the other hand cohabitation, divorce and remarriage have become increasingly, if reluctantly, accepted. Some sociologists now discuss the possibility of three types of marriage, the first for romance, the second for parenting, the third for companionship. Renewable marriage licences for a limited time of five or ten years have become a serious suggestion, particularly in America, where 39 per cent of married couples divorce within five years. Alvin Toffler, author of *Future Shock*, predicted in 1970 that serial

marriages would become a 'regrettable necessity'.

Moses seemed to have come to a similar conclusion when he allowed divorce because of the hardness of the people's hearts, although Jesus sharply reminded his listeners that this was not the ideal. He would have been only too well aware of the devastation left in the wake of broken relationships, and the tremendous need for healing that came as a result of broken covenants and broken homes.

The future of marriage

It is not so much that 'the family' is under threat. However fragmented our family network may be, most of us have mothers, brothers, grandparents, second cousins, someone, somewhere in the background to whom we can relate, or retreat, when necessary. What *is* at risk is marriage. That permanent, exclusive, male/female partnership is taking a rough battering at the moment. Relaxation of the divorce laws and sexual conduct, unemployment and female independence have created a situation where people want, and can obtain a way out, and where many others are asking 'Why go in?'.

Those concerned about the future consequences can only warn 'You ain't seen nothing yet', in terms of the stress this is likely to create. We are going to need an army of counsellors, therapists, psychiatrists, social workers, child guidance clinics to sort it all out.

What is going to happen to the generation of males demoralized and emasculated by the effects of unemployment? The television series *Boys from the Blackstuff* spelt out some of the intolerable strains unemployment places on a marriage relationship. We stand in great danger of reducing men to the level of drones, kicked out by their female counterparts when they no longer have a productive part to play, and become a drain on resources.

No wonder few male prophets wish to abolish marriage entirely. The alternatives have so many deficiencies in comparison. They lack security, permanency, stability, commitment, responsibility; the very qualities which are at the centre of a good marriage. When these are missing, adults flounder from one disastrous substitute to another, and children are left feeling bewildered and betrayed. Those concerned that the major victims of divorce are invariably the children are putting forward the idea that those undertaking parental marriage should be prepared to accept a minimum commitment of fifteen years.

So many of the problems facing families come back to the central relationship between the adults. If that is threatened, the ripples spread in ever increasing circles. An article in *New Society* dated April 1982 by Helen Chappell ('Not the marrying kind') suggested that rather than replacing marriage we should learn to improve the character of it. Marriage may no longer be the goal of every woman, and many would like to see changes in the marriage relationship, but most female prophets are still pro-marriage.

Although marriage rates may be falling, the proportion of 'ever married' remains high. The sociologist Jessie Bernard concludes that marriage has as secure a future as any other human social form. Men and women want and need intimacy, reassurance, affection, unity. There will continue to be commitment, even if the word marriage is replaced by 'pair bond'. When we express concern about the future of marriage, we are really asking about future controls on sexual behaviour.

Freedom or licence?
Will standards become so permissive that marriage will become obsolete, or does society need to regulate sexual relationships in order to survive?.

Do we confuse freedom with licence? What about the casualties produced by the emphasis on self fulfilment?

What are the purposes of traditional standards of behaviour? Are they still relevant? When values such as love, trust, reliability and faithfulness are cheapened, should we be surprised if people are no longer able to sustain relationships? Do people really want a society where 'anything goes'?

Not such a permissive society

According to popular opinion (Mirror Survey, July 1982) people are cautious about getting married, but once they are married they expect it to be permanent. 'Marriage is seen as the nucleus of a lifetime within which a family may grow,' concluded a more up-market survey (*Options*, Special Survey Part 1). People may be prepared to accept a casual living arrangement if there are no children. When children put in an appearance both society and one, or both, partners are likely to become more concerned about a more secure relationship. 'The strength of a whole and healthy family unit is still our greatest barrier against disaster,' wrote Claire Shepherd in *Woman's Realm*. 'Our psychiatric hospitals are full of people without that barrier.'

Unfortunately there are an increasing number likely to be very much 'at risk' in that case. How do you start to build a few defences with them? What do you say to the girl who has had three babies and three abortions, and is distraught because she is now expecting her fourth child by her present 'feller', and the hospital has refused to sterilize her because she is too young? What factors have led to her lifestyle? How do you begin to reach through to her needs? What images of 'family', what future are her children growing into?

What is a family?

How do you define family in a society where the traditional image of mother and father and rosy faced children can no longer be safely assumed? Rapoport and Rapoport report that in the USA 'probably more than half (of all children) will have lived in a family different from the traditional nuclear type for a significant period of their early lives' (*Working Couples*).

The dictionary defines family as 'parents, children, servants, forming (a) household', and 'set of parents and children or of relations, group of related people'. Has our view of the family become too limited, too restrictive? In the Old Testament there is no word to correspond with the traditional view of family as father, mother and children. The nearest it gets is reference to household, clan, tribe. In the New Testament the 'household' would probably include the male head, his wife, children, slaves and dependants. Those within strong family networks still see it as a 'developing interdependent group of parents and children surrounded by a comforting cushion of grandparents, aunts, uncles and cousins'. Others, aware that the everyday reality for many can be very different from that define it as a group, or unit, which may be related by blood, but can also be extended by adoption, amalgamation, self selection or common interest. Units as small as one parent with dependent children are included in this definition despite strong pressure from some quarters to confine the use of the word family to the conventional model.

When is a family not a family?

As the female head of a one-parent family I can identify with the hurt and bewilderment such judgements convey. There is no need to tell those who do not conform to the traditional pattern they are lacking a vital factor. They know that only too well. A Catholic priest in a downtown area in Liverpool no longer dares to preach on the 'ideal family', because of the number of suicides and cases of depression likely to follow such an attempt. Do our attitudes/reactions push the 'bruised reeds' of our society even nearer to the breaking point, or show them something of the Father who understands their problems, who knows all about the sense of loss, rejection, powerlessness, the struggle to survive, who loves them as his own 'little children'.

It seems strange that Christians can talk so freely about the family of God, yet suffer some kind of spiritual apoplexy at the idea that a step-parent or single parent should slot into the concept of 'family'. Would it be more constructive if we were to concentrate less on condemning people for deficiencies in their family support system, and more on remedying the situation?

When the family unit has fallen apart for some reason people are going to need help and support to put their lives back together again — especially when children are involved. It is sad to hear those who do not fit the accepted stereotype complaining that folk in church seem to have great difficulty understanding their situation, or even acknowledging their existence. Ferdinand Mount states that 'A blood family which does not acknowledge or exercise responsibility has ceased to be more than a family in name. Conversely, a group of persons not related by blood who do exercise such responsibilities can come to be described as a family.'

Is your fellowship fulfilling this function for those who need the warmth of love and acceptance, and the enabling of some form of back-up system?

The family or families?

For individual families the key to whether or not the function of a family is being fulfilled seems to lie in the depth of commitment, and the acceptance of responsibility. As in scripture there is no one model of the 'family' but an infinite variety of families. In today's society there may be four generation families, reconstituted families, families where both parents are working, one-parent families, and families living in community. Even inside the 'traditional' family there will be enormous varieties in priorities and attitudes, towards work, education, leisure, finance, and relationships. As there has always been. The leisured lady of the Victorian middle classes led a very different existence from her working class counterpart.

With rare exceptions families reflect the culture in which they are placed. The multiple problems of the families in East London can be largely attributed to high unemployment, poor housing conditions, isolation and urbanization, just as the polygamous networks of the Old Testament were a product of the bitter struggle for survival in a semi-desert nomadic society.

Acceptance or alienation?

Then success or failure depended not only on family and social structures but on whether the individuals within those structures heard and obeyed the word of God, and set his values to work in relationships. When they got things right, the results were powerful and enduring. When they got it wrong, households became claustrophobic and divisive. But even in the worst conditions where there were those who were prepared to listen and learn God was able to work to redeem the situation. In a society which is becoming ever more divided between rich and poor, old and young, those who have received Christian teaching and those to whom it has never been made comprehensible (or relevant) there is an urgent need for God's representatives to listen and learn from him and those who are alienated from him. For too long those inside the churches have been sitting halfheartedly beckoning outsiders in to them, instead of getting alongside them, identifying their needs, and drawing them step by step into the security of God's love. If we pass superficial value judgements without fully appreciating the limitations and pressures many people have to contend with daily, we are as guilty as those Jesus condemned for straining a gnat, and swallowing a camel.

'What is required is a recognition of the complexity of contemporary issues, a readiness to accept that there are likely to be different ways of dealing with them, and a cultivation of the capacity to work with and resolve problems of living as parents in today's society,' wrote Rapoport and Rapoport in *Fathers, Mothers and Others*. The same applies to problems in male/female relationships, care of the elderly, conflicts within the church family, or wherever else there are individuals learning to relate to one another.

Passing the buck
It is possible to argue indefinitely about the causes of present day pressures on families. Male and female, parents and professionals, left and right, liberal and fundamentalist all have different perspectives and analyses. One side see social conditions as the result of all ills, another the Government, another sin, or the fallibility of human nature.

Whatever the causes one thing is certain, something is drastically wrong. A priest in affluent Solihull said that one half of the pastoral care in his parish is dealing with problems of family life. Those working in the inner city, or on large housing estates would probably put the figure much higher. In the concluding pages of *Fathers, Mothers and Others* Rapoport and Rapoport state 'The reality of contemporary life points to the impression that many ordinary families are in trouble…'.

A whole combination of factors have led to the erosion of family life, and those concerned to redress the balance need to be thinking about a long-term commitment. The problems are not going to be solved overnight or even in a couple of decades. Neither are they going to be solved unless there is more partnership, rather than the usual polarization. As long as the family continues to be used as a political football — by religious leaders, or politicians, or individuals inside the family unit — there is hardly likely to be much improvement in the situation.

Being involved

Weeping and wailing and gnashing of teeth will not heal broken homes and wounded lives. Those who have earned the right to speak out are those who have rolled up their sleeves, and got on with the job at hand. Many Christian groups have the experience and authority of centuries of involvement, or 'picking up the pieces'. No one need look far to find positive tasks, in their own family, church, community.

'We don't seem to meet the problems you do,' said a middle-class gentleman from a select suburb. Even given the vastly different social conditions I could only conclude he went around with his eyes and ears permanently shut. Wherever there are people in relationship there are going to be problems. We are all individuals. Our backgrounds, personalities, priorities are different. How far families are able to negotiate the inevitable clashes is the factor determining whether they survive or split. If Christian families could show the world that there is a power stronger than our individual wills, and weaknesses that would speak far more powerfully than any sermon. It was left to the Christians to set an example of family life in the promiscuity and infidelity of Philippi, Rome and Corinth. The need to see and experience 'positive models', particularly for those from negative family experiences, lays a heavy responsibility on all who believe in the value of family life. This does not mean perpetrating the myth that Christian families need to be images of perfection. We are all flawed, and failure can lead to new self understanding and possibility of growth. Often this may involve seeking outside help... if only on the level of 'blowing your top' to a well trusted friend. 'We need to dispel the idea that only some need help,' said a parent with both feet firmly on the ground. 'It should be as natural to go to somewhere to talk about problems as to go to the dentist.'

Sharing with other parents might also help us to get less 'wound up' by the imperfections in our children, and see their conflicts as an inevitable part of the growing up process. Two teenagers were clashing about the use of their study bedroom. One needed to revise for exams, the other wanted to use the record player. Neither would accept a compromise solution. In the end there was an almighty punch-up, which frightened everyone involved, but the lessons it taught were invaluable. Learning to negotiate, to see the other person's needs, to admit mistakes, is always painful, but it is part of the 'give and take' that is necessary in any set of relationships.

Emphasis on the family
The present emphasis on the family is equally distressing for single people or those struggling with the painful aftermath of divorce or separation. 'If I hear another sermon about the family I shall scream,' said a divorced man. Such hurt is understandable, but if marriage and family life are one of the 'burning issues' of our day how can it not form a major part of the teaching programme of the local church? If we can set our own house in order surely we stand a greater chance of helping others to get theirs sorted out?

Encouragement
There is terrific need for a 'ministry of encouragement'
both inside and outside the Church today. Some Christians
are too fond of telling others what they shouldn't be doing,
rather than seeing the good things, and building on those.
The pat on the back can achieve far more than a rap over
the knuckles. 'We need to capitalize on the good, rather
than assuming the worst,' said a social worker. When there
are differences in cultural values and attitudes this is particularly relevant.

Acknowledging change
Certain sections of the Church seem unable to cope with
anything other than complete conformity, and have little
appreciation of the diversity of human nature, or the
changes that have taken place in the family, in society, and
in women. We stand in great danger of missing out on many
potential areas of growth if we ignore the challenging and
uncomfortable, and push people into a mould which relies
heavily on one partner doing all the giving, and the other all
the taking. One factor which emerged strongly from the
recent survey by Gallup for Birds Eye was the need for
separate identity and independence for all members within
the family unit.

Those extolling the virtues of the 'traditional family' need
to consider the claim that it has become 'a ghetto for twenty
to thirty-year-olds', demanding the individual's whole love
and interest. Is it a bastion against the world, or a psychological and emotional pressure cooker, with divorce replacing death as the safety valve? Should families be encouraged to function as individual units within a wider
framework? Can they be freed from assumptions and traditions that stunt individual growth and restrict their ability to
reach out to others?

Assessment
The complex problems of the twentieth century will not be
solved by a naive belief that we can 'put the clock back'. We
need to question and evaluate the various philosophies and

pronouncements that pour from the presses, including the Christian ones. Many so called 'Christian' standards or concepts are simply cultural hangovers from a previous century. Political statements deserve a healthy scepticism too. Is it pure coincidence that government concern about the value of the family and woman's role in the home coincides with a shrinking labour market, and cuts in all the social services? Should we sit back and allow any government to cost the effect of their policies purely in financial terms, and with little regard for the social and psychological consequences?

Such issues cannot be ignored if we are to find some constructive ways forward. With one in three marriages ending in divorce no one can afford to be complacent.

New realism

Neither should we be tempted to believe the situation is irredeemable. There are signs of a new realism creeping into the writings and discussions about marriage and family life. Topics such as communication and conflict, managing your emotions, and love and anger in marriage could help to counteract the unrealistic expectations that encourage couples to believe their marriage is a failure.

Certainly we have to do some long hard thinking about the shift of power in the marriage relationship, and the male's contribution to parenting. A lot of concern is expressed about single-parent families when an enormous number of so-called conventional families are operating as if there was only one parent. The slogan 'Families need fathers' is just as relevant to many units where some form of marriage still exists as it is for those broken by divorce. Parenting is a joint responsibility, not a female prerogative. It is demanding, time consuming, expensive and long term, and the sooner the glamour and dishonesty surrounding it are stripped off the better. Parents need more support and preparation for this increasingly tough task.

In the same way we need to realize the true cost of divorce. I have been researching into marriage and divorce for more than a decade, and I have not discovered many

people falling apart as a result of faithfulness and permanence. On the other hand I have met, and read about, an
enormous number of people who are torn by jealousy, guilt,
insecurity and bitterness as a result of infidelity and imper-
manence.

Families in fashion

Whether the permissive society will be replaced by one completely without sexual restrictions, or by a swing back to a
more puritanical era remains to be seen but the anti-family
propaganda of the sixties seems to have been replaced by a
resurgence of interest in the family. All the major political
parties pay at least lip service to the value of the family, and
pressure is being applied for the need for family impact
statements and a family perspective in policy making.
Family Forum and the Study Commission on the Family are
two bodies researching, analysing and reporting on matters affecting the family and a Minister for the Family is a
serious possibility. Women's magazines with 'family values'
are coming back into fashion, and there is growing belief
that people are heartily sick of endless talk about sex.
Recent research from the USA indicates a return to the
family with young executives refusing moves and unsocial
hours, and demanding flexitime in order to be more available for their families. In this country public interest in the
Royal baby and the family affairs of all the Royals remains
as high as ever, and politicians and church leaders can
quickly fall from grace if they tarnish the image of the
happy family man.

The book *A Fairer Future for Children* by Mia Kellmer
Pringle (Macmillan, 1980) suggests that the middle-class
professional groups are settling down to weather the storm,
and that the respectable working class have been more affected by technological change than anti-family teaching.
The family is also seen as the most beneficial support system
for the poor and disadvantaged.

A recent poll revealed that most people's needs are still
best met within the family. Considering all the attacks on it
during the last two decades the family 'appears to be

stronger and more viable than many anticipated' (R.M. Moroney, *The Family and the State*, Longman, 1976).

In need of support networks

It is no use relying on a false optimism, or clinging to the belief that the family will survive whatever happens, though. Because of the pressures working against it we need much more effective and efficient back-up systems. This could be in one to one relationships, where people are prepared to spend time, to listen, to encourage, especially those most 'at risk'. It may be through groups which have grown from identification of a need, and the desire to reach out to others. It may be through political or educational influence. Books, papers, TV programmes, new courses in relationships and survival skills can all help to spread positive models, and challenge false assumptions. New initiatives to aid the elderly, and unemployed are desperately needed. Isolation is an enormous problem in a society where living units are separated into individual boxes. So many people have little or no contact with the wider community.

'We need to discover ways of ministry which create community, which make space for people to grow in mutual trust and concern,' said David Randall, writing in the *Church Observer*, September 1982.

There are indications of new life, of renewal, of the re-awakening of communities, but sadly the Church too often remains shut in on itself. There are still many Christians who are afraid that involvement with the world could still mean getting their hands dirty, especially if 'politics' should inadvertently raise it ugly head.

A friend described Christianity as 'the biggest club in the world'. He reckoned wherever he went he could get a bed or a meal. That is excellent, providing it does not exclude those unable to articulate their Christianity in the 'in' terms. Real warmth and love are very attractive qualities, and speak volumes to a very needy world. Those whose own family links are fairly tenuous, through distance or division, find terrific strength from belonging to God's family.

'The local church has become my family now,' said a woman whose marriage had recently ended in divorce. When my husband was dying our family felt as if we were bolstered up on a great wave of love with letters, prayers, phone calls, financial help, offers of holidays, and practical and emotional support from Christians all over the country. The day before he came out of hospital he had twenty-six visitors. In contrast the man in the next bed had one friend who called in occasionally the entire length of his stay in hospital. When he went home it was to an empty flat. There are dozens of people like him in every town and village in our land. How can we start extending our Christian networks to reach through to their need of love and care? If we feel lonely, under pressure, cut off from family and community, how can we start establishing our own networks? How do we get beyond waiting for someone to reach through to us, and realize they may be just as desperate for someone to reach through to them? So many of our social contacts are on a superficial level. Could we get away from the 'How are you? Fine, thank you' routine? Would we know how to respond if someone actually broke the expected pattern and revealed their true feelings? Dare we? Admitting a need is never easy, especially for those schooled in the stiff upper lip tradition, but it is surprising how quickly barriers begin to crumble, and how relieved the other person may be to realize it is safe and acceptable to talk about the things that have been bugging them. By priding ourselves on our independence and self sufficiency we may be depriving ourselves of a great deal of practical and emotional support, and failing to see the enormous potential that could be released into society if people could be encouraged to acknowledge and share their abilities and skills.

The future in balance
The future of the family, and society, is in the balance. The pamphlet *Marriage and the Family in Britain Today* (CIO) reminds us that 'The pattern of caring love, of give and take which characterizes the ordinary family points towards the shape of the good society.' Will that pattern disintegrate

completely with couples moving through a series of ephemeral unions, sticking together as long as it pleases them, and opting out when the going gets tough. Will the present diversity of family styles remain, or will one begin to emerge as a significant form? Can the needs of children (and men), and the rights of women be negotiated sufficiently to restore a balanced relationship? Will marriage continue to be seen as a poor deal for women? Will future developments in technology prove the final nail in the coffin of the family? In his book *The Third Wave* Alvin Toffler predicts the contrary. He foresees a future in which new technology will restore work to the home and reunite the family. The home would become a central unit of society with increased medical economic and social functions and families would become reintegrated into the community.

It sounds good, if you are riding the crest of the information technology wave. If you are one of the pebbles being severely battered by the onslaught, it looks less optimistic. David Lyon, a researcher and lecturer in social analysis, suggests that the new technology could become a tool to be used creatively and responsibly or a tyrant sweeping everything before it. If future family patterns depend more on decisions we make about work and technology than on pulpit pounding, what future are we helping to shape?

The future in our hands
'This is a time for us to take chances,' wrote Mia Kellmer Pringle in *A Fairer Future for Children*. 'To try out ideas and welcome criticism which may take our thinking a step forward into the future... The future is not decided in advance, we are continually making it. We are currently entering a rare open moment in history, a space into which we can insert our wills.' The Rapoports also talk about being at 'a pivotal point in history.. in which new models of family life itself and the relation between family and society are required' (*Fathers, Mothers and Others*). They believe these models are already being worked out by parents, with or without the experts.

How aware are you/your church of the two most crucial

issues facing western society? Are you working out a
theology of work and the family? If so, is it dictated by a
desire to maintain the *status quo*, or working for human liberation, the desire to see 'God's new creation in every social
structure'? (*The Future of Partnership*, Letty Russell,
Westminster Press, 1979). Alvin Toffler believes that 'Most
of us are already engaged in either resisting — or creating
the new civilization' (*The Third Wave*). What part are you
playing? It is no use sitting on our backsides bewailing the
mess people are making of their own lives, and those
around them, if we have nothing better to offer them. Of
course the world takes no notice if our pronouncements are
empty talk. If they can be shown to work, if Christian
families had such love and respect for one another they
could build a firm nucleus from which to reach out to
others, people might begin to ask what's happening. So
many are desperate for meaning, guidelines. They need
lights to shine out in the dark world; people who can speak
with authority, not to dominate, but to present a viable alternative.

Tackling the opposition
For too long the Church/Christians have lacked confidence.
We have let the opposition have it too much his own way.
There has been a deluge of novels, plays, films, perpetrating philosophies diametrically opposed to the Christian
doctrine of concern for the individual. If the media is 'central to the communication of options/alternate lifestyles'
(*Marriage and Alternatives*), how many prayer groups are
down on their knees beseeching God for Christian writers,
producers, programme directors with the impossible task
of pushing upstream against such a raging torrent? Do we
challenge the values pushed into our homes and minds
night after night, or let them lap over us deceiving ourselves
we will not be influenced? When those around us discuss
issues which Christians should be concerned about are we
stuck for an opinion, or ready to counter-attack? Is the
Church/Christians standing out and demanding a voice? Is
it/are we a power to be reckoned with, or a squeak of protest

from the sidelines? Can we get beyond the trivialities and back to the rudiments of the gospel?

Jesus spoke with authority because he sat where the people sat. He listened to their problems, and understood their needs. He didn't preach at them. He told them stories they could identify with. He was not only aware of the great divide between the people and their God, he did all within his power to bring the two together. Do we know where God's lost ones are today? Do we care? Are we seeking to lead them gently nearer to where they could be?

Bearing one another's burdens
'You feel so guilty,' said one of our acquaintances, 'when you look at the needs of the world. What can one person do?' If he had stopped to evaluate his own life he would have realized that his contribution went far beyond the one child from the Third World that he and his family were sponsoring, and who was making them so aware of the reality of other people's situations. What influence do/could you have, in your own family, at work, in your leisure pursuits, in your local involvement, with your voting powers? Do our activities and attitudes ease or aggravate the pressures on our own, and other families? 'If I can only help one person it will be worthwhile,' said a lady from the Mothers' Union, who had obviously done far more than that in her long and active concern for the families in her neighbourhood.

Meetings, organizations, committees may have their right and proper place, but they are no substitute for the influence each of us can have on those surrounding us. The one to one contact is still the most effective. How many golden opportunities do we pass over each day? A casual, or serious word? A smile? A prayer? A hug? How seriously do we take the responsibility to act as godparents, or best man? Is it a formality, or a continuing commitment?

So many people are overwhelmed by the pressures of our fragmented and fear-ridden society. How long will we continue to hope that the Government, or the voluntary organizations, or social services will come up with the

panacea for all ills? Of course they have a part, and a very
important part, to play. So do we. Families are made up of
people, young mothers (and fathers), elderly parents,
teenagers, the unemployed, the over-employed. However
isolated our circumstances may be, most of us come into
contact with other individuals at some stage. What skill,
ability, expertise can you share? What lessons have you
learned, particularly the painful ones? How good are you at
listening, at helping to bear the other person's burden?
When my husband died a huge number of people experienced a terrific sense of loss. Not only did they miss his
vitality, administrative expertise and his outrageous sense
of fun, what really hurt was the feeling they had lost someone who was concerned and interested in them. 'However
trivial the matter you brought to him he made you feel as if
he cared about you,' said one of his colleagues.

Re-presenting Christ

We can become so preoccupied with the message we forget
that we are the message. Does the world see Christ in us,
however dim the reflection? Do we hug him selfishly against
our own needs, or by sharing ourselves bring him back into
the world which rightly belongs to him? 'I'm so confused,'
said a girl who had been battered in turn by a spiritualist, a
Jehovah's witness, and a South American evangelist. 'I wish
they all believed the same thing.'

What is the essence of the gospel, the good news? How do
we interpret it to her, and so many others who are desperate
for some hope, some strength, to help them cope with their
family situations? How can we communicate 'God loves you.
You are important to him' in language people will understand? How can we reach through to them? 'We are all hurt
by past experience', said a preacher recently. We all carry
with us feelings of guilt, failure, bitterness, rejection, insecurity. They may stem from bereavement, broken marriages, inadequate or misguided parents, a whole host of
factors that have made us what we are. 'There is a need in
every individual to be acknowledged and confirmed by
others,' said Anthony Mann in *The Human Paradox*

(National Marriage Guidance Council, 1974). 'To be wanted and accepted is a need that persists throughout life.'

Whether we begin to meet those needs, in our homes, and in the wider community, could determine not only if there is a future for the family but also if there is a future for humanity.

Bibliography

The Family and Marriage in Britain, Ronald Fletcher, Pelican, 1973

The Future of Marriage, Jessie Bernard, Souvenir, 1972

The Family in Transition, Jeanne Hinton, National Centre for Christian Communities and Networks

Happy Families, Study Commission on the Family, 1980

Families in Focus, Lesley Rimmer, Study Commission on the Family, 1981

Families and How to Survive Them, John Cleese and Robin Skynner, Methuen, 1983

Marriage, Faith and Love, Jack Dominian, Darton, Longman & Todd, 1981

The Human Paradox, Antony Mann, National Marriage Guidance Council, 1974

Fathers, Mothers and Others, Rapoport and Rapoport, Routledge & Kegan Paul, 1977

Ourselves and our Children, Boston Women's Health Book Collective, Penguin, 1981

The Price of Loving, Jane Davies, Mowbray, 1981

A Fairer Future for Children, Mia Kellmer Pringle, Macmillan, 1980

The Feminine Mystique, Betty Friedan, Penguin, 1965

The Second Stage, Betty Friedan, Michael Joseph, 1982

Dispossessed Daughters of Eve, Susan Dowell and Linda Hurcombe, SCM, 1981

Not in God's Image, ed. Julia O'Faolain, Virago, 1979

Flesh of my Flesh, Una Kroll, Darton, Longman & Todd, 1975

Index